CRAZY HORSE
and
KORCZAK

THE STORY OF AN EPIC MOUNTAIN CARVING

By
Robb DeWall

Illustrations By
Marinka Ziolkowski

Published By
Korczak's Heritage, Inc.
Crazy Horse, South Dakota 57730

ON THE COVER

CRAZY HORSE SILHOUETTE
Korczak Ziolkowski, Sc.
1/2-inch steel plate   1962
Dimensions:
  15½ feet high
  23 feet wide
Entrance to Crazy Horse Memorial
Black Hills of South Dakota

FIRST EDITION: May 3, 1982
Second printing: January, 1983

Copyright ©1982 by Korczak Ziolkowski, Sc.
Library of Congress Catalog Card Number   NB237.Z5D4

Published by Korczak's Heritage, Inc.
Crazy Horse, South Dakota 57730

Printed in the United States of America
By Modern Press, Inc.
Sioux Falls, South Dakota

The text of this book is set in Cheltenham type.

Library of Congress Cataloging in Publication Data

DeWall, Robb
  Crazy Horse and Korczak.

  Bibliography: p. 152
  Includes index.

   1. Ziolkowski, Korczak, 1908-1982—Juvenile
literature.   2. Sculptors—United States—Biography—Juvenile
literature.   3. Crazy Horse, ca. 1842-1877—Portraits,
etc.—Juvenile literature.   4. Dakota Indians—Pictorial works—
Juvenile literature.   5. Dakota Indians—History—Juvenile
literature. [1. Ziolkowski, Korczak, 1908-
2. Sculptors.   3. Crazy Horse, ca. 1842-1877.   4. Dakota
Indians.   5. Indians of North America—South Dakota]
I. Ziolkowski, Marinka, ill. II. Title
NB237.Z5D4   730'.92'4   [B]   [92]   82-7726
                                                      AACR2

AUTHOR'S NOTE

On October 20, 1982, as the second printing of this book was being planned, Korczak, aged 74, passed on very unexpectedly. As he discusses in this book, he knew from the outset his colossal Crazy Horse project is larger than any one man's lifetime; thus, he prepared detailed plans for the mountain carving and the humanitarian aspects of Crazy Horse. His wife, Ruth, and their large family are dedicated to carrying on his work.

The text of this book is unchanged from the First Edition.

ABOUT THIS BOOK

The following story is based on fact. Every year Korczak Ziolkowski, sculptor of Crazy Horse Memorial in the Black Hills of South Dakota, receives scores of letters from students of all ages.

Younger students often have learned of the sculptor and his work through *My Weekly Reader* of current events, which is studied in many grade school classrooms in the United States. Others learn of him from the print and broadcast media which have told the story of the Crazy Horse mountain carving around the world.

This book attempts to answer many of the questions the sculptor receives from those students.

Tom Whitney, the boy who visits Crazy Horse in this story, and his family are fictional characters, but they are representative of the millions of people who have visited Crazy Horse since its dedication June 3, 1948. The stories Tom and his family are told and the things they see and do in this story are factual.

A chronology of the major events in the progress of Crazy Horse Memorial appears at the back of this book. Readers of this volume also might enjoy some of the books listed in the bibliography; all are recommended by Korczak.

The author would like to express his gratitude to the many people who helped in the preparation of this book. Special thanks to Jessie Sundstrom, for invaluable help in editing the manuscript.

Robb DeWall
Crazy Horse, 1982

ABOUT THE ILLUSTRATOR

Marinka Ziolkowski is the youngest daughter of Crazy Horse Sculptor and Mrs. Korczak Ziolkowski. She developed an interest in drawing at an early age, and plans to pursue a career in commercial art. This is her first book of illustrations, published when she was 18 years old.

TABLE OF CONTENTS

PHOTOGRAPHS

(Pictures of Korczak's sculpture were taken by the sculptor)

LIST OF ILLUSTRATIONS

Nothing lasts long—
only the Earth
and the Mountains.

White Antelope

CHAPTER 1

TOM'S ASSIGNMENT

Spring fever was the order of the day—the last of school. Through the wide open windows of Mr. Johnson's classroom the students could hear the sounds of splashing in the new birdbath and smell the lilacs budding on the hedge around the schoolyard. It would have been a great day to play hooky, except report cards were due out at noon.

Tom Whitney was daydreaming about Indians. He was a good student who hardly ever daydreamed, but today was an exception. At noon his parents were picking him up to begin their summer vacation in the Black Hills of South Dakota where they were going to visit the Crazy Horse mountain carving.

Crazy Horse had a special meaning to the class. In studying about the West, the students had become very interested in Indians. They had read about the mountain carving last year in *My Weekly Reader* of current events, and had written to Crazy Horse for more information.

That's how Tom came to suggest the paper drive as a class fund-raising project for Crazy Horse, and why he was daydreaming about Indians today.

His attention was drawn back to the classroom as Mr. Johnson was saying, ". . . so before we hear what each of you is going to do during summer vacation, let's be sure Tom knows what we want him to find out for us about Crazy Horse when he visits there."

The teacher was very popular with the students. He was an athletic man in his mid-30's who also served as one of the school's coaches. The students liked his sense of humor. He walked over to their bulletin board covered with Crazy

1

Horse materials, and took down a letter on yellow stationery. "Let's read again what Korczak wrote to Tom. Maybe you'd read it to us, Tom?"

The boy was so excited about his upcoming visit to the mountain carving he wasn't even nervous walking up in front of the class. He was a rather skinny four and one-half foot tall youth with dark eyes and dark hair that seemed to have a mind of its own. Tom didn't like to read in class, but this was his favorite letter. His only other letters were from his grandmother. Blushing just a little, the boy cleared his throat and started to read.

"Louder," someone said.

Tom started again:

Tom reads Korczak's letter to the class

Crazy Horse Mt.
Avenue of the Chiefs
Crazy Horse, South Dakota 57730

Dear Mr. Whitney:

Thank you very much for your letter and for those of your classmates. I want you to know how much we appreciate the interest of your class the last two years and your help with the Crazy Horse mountain carving. Your efforts are very meaningful to me.

We were very pleased to receive the check for $40 your class sent last year and the additional $85 you sent this year. You and your classmates must have worked very hard to collect so many old newspapers to sell for recycling. We have written special thanks to your teacher, Mr. Johnson, for helping your

2

class coordinate this big project and for hauling the papers in his pickup to the recycling plant in the nearby town.

The article you enclosed from your local newspaper reporting about your class project also was most interesting.

Summer is a very busy time for us here. We have many visitors from all over the world. My sons and I are working on the mountain carving during the good weather months, so I am not able to take the time to meet many visitors. But, since you will be visiting Crazy Horse with your family right after school is out, I would be pleased to meet you as a representative of your class, which has worked so hard to help Crazy Horse. We always enjoy having young people here because this is a project for the future.

Please let us know approximately when you will arrive, and we'll look forward to seeing you.

Very sincerely,
Korczak Ziolkowski, sculptor

Tom blushed as he stumbled over the sculptor's long name, and told the class as he returned to his seat, "I still don't know how to pronounce that. It's hard to say."

"It's pronounced CÓRE-JOCK JEWEL-CÚFF-SKI. That's how they say it on TV," said Gary Laskowski in his loud voice. "It's a Polish name. His parents were Polish. They died when he was little."

"That's right, Gary," smiled Mr. Johnson. "I seem to recall your grandparents are Polish."

"He's always bragging about it," said several boys together.

"Well, Americans come from many nationalities, as we've studied. We all can be proud of our own ancestry, just as the American Indian can be proud of his heritage and culture," said the teacher. "Yes, Jinny?"

"I'd like to know how he learned to be a sculptor," said the little blond girl whose hand had been up. She liked to draw, and everyone thought she drew the best in the class.

Susan, who sat next to Tom, said, "I think we should make a list of questions so he won't forget." She knew boys often forgot things.

"It would be like an assignment," someone else said.

Mr. Johnson looked at Tom, and asked, "Would that be a good idea, Tom? A little list for you? That way we can all be sure our questions are answered."

Tom didn't want any list, but he didn't want to forget either. He answered reluctantly, "A list would be okay."

"All right, let's make a list. Maybe we should put it on the blackboard. Who'd like to write for us? How about . . . Jeff? You need the practice I think."

The students laughed. They knew Jeff had the best penmanship in the class.

Alice had her hand up, and when Mr. Johnson called on her, she said, "I want to know about the feather. How can he make that feather up there on top of a mountain?"

3

Mr. Johnson picked up the small white model of Crazy Horse Mrs. Ziolkowski had sent them. "Yes, that feather looks quite unusual. Make that number two, Jeff. How to make the feather? Number one is Jinny's question: how did he become a sculptor?"

Dick said, "I'd like to know about the rock. Those pieces of rock blasted off the mountain that Mrs. Ziolkowski sent us are very colorful. My brother took mine. He collects rocks, and wants to know about all the minerals in that rock."

Jeff wrote that on the blackboard as number three.

Heather said, "I want to know why he named his bulldozer *Zeus*. That's a funny name for a bulldozer." Several students agreed.

As Jeff wrote, Mr. Johnson said, "I think one of the main things Tom can ask the sculptor is why he's carving the mountain. Maybe Tom can find out more about that for us."

Robert said, "My father says he doesn't know why it should be Crazy Horse."

Mr. Johnson responded, "Yes, that's a good point. Why Crazy Horse instead of another Indian leader?"

Jeff screeched the chalk on the blackboard and everybody winced.

Cindy, sitting in the corner, raised her hand half way up. She was very shy, and didn't talk much in class.

"Yes, Cindy? What would you like to put on the list?" asked the teacher.

"The children. They have 10 children. I'd like to know more about them. It must be fun to live in the West and have a mountain carving to an Indian."

"That would be very interesting to know about. We'll put that on Tom's assignment list. I'll bet you get to meet some of those children, Tom."

Dan, whose father was a banker, raised his hand. "We don't understand why he won't take any money from the government. We read he turned down millions of dollars. And, I'd like to know what happens to the money we sent. We sent $40 last year and $85 this year. That's a lot of money."

Smiling, Mr. Johnson said, "Fine question. Why refuse government money? Any other questions?"

Gary's voice filled the room. "I want to know what Crazy Horse is pointing at!"

"A very good question. Gary, we can hear you very well. Write a little faster, Jeff. You don't have to draw the letters, just write them."

Pat said, "I saw Korczak on the TV show, and I'd like to know why he has that great big beard. It's about the biggest beard I ever saw. Does it keep him warm on the mountain? I'd like to know about that."

"Okay. What else? Anything else, class? Jim?"

"That was a really big blast on the mountain we saw on the TV show. I'd like to know how he makes those blasts."

"Well, we have quite a list. Eleven questions so far. Connie, would you read the list for us?"

A tall, skinny red-haired girl stood up and read the list. There were 11 questions:

4

1. How become a sculptor
2. How make the feather
3. What minerals in the rock
4. Why *Zeus*
5. Why carving a mountain
6. Why Crazy Horse
7. About children
8. Why turn down government money
9. What Crazy Horse pointing at
10. Why the big beard
11. How make a blast

"Thank you, Connie. You read that very well. Any other questions to put on Tom's list?"

David said, "We've read that he says Crazy Horse is in the mountain. I'd like to ask him how he knows Crazy Horse is in that mountain."

"I'll bet he has quite an answer for that one," said Mr. Johnson, nodding to Jeff to add that to the list.

"Well, Tom, I guess that's your assignment. A dozen good questions, and I'll bet you have a lot more yourself. It should be quite an exciting visit. I know we're all looking forward to hearing all about Crazy Horse after school starts again next fall.

"Now, let's hear about what some others of you will be doing all summer. Who wants to be first?"

The class spent the rest of the time before report cards talking about the summer ahead. Tom had a hard time concentrating as he wondered what it was going to be like at Crazy Horse.

Finally, the report cards were handed out. Tom barely glanced at his as he dashed outside looking for his parents. When he found their station wagon, he started chattering about his list as he climbed in the back seat beside his little blonde sister, Carole.

They were off to the Black Hills.

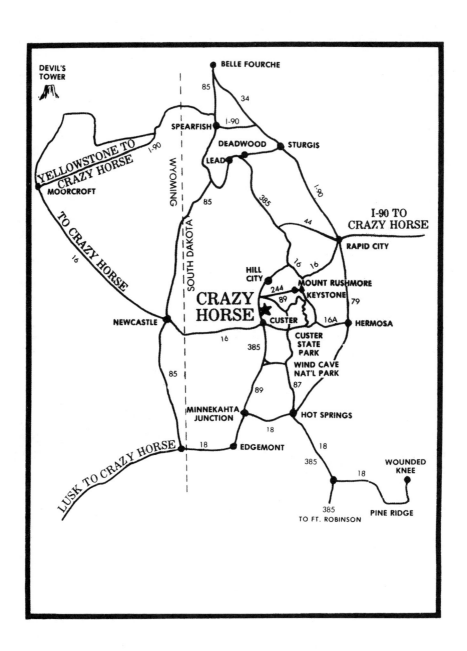

CHAPTER 2

ARRIVAL AT CRAZY HORSE

"Daddy, look at the gold-colored mountain!" exclaimed Carole as they approached Crazy Horse on a beautiful summer morning a few days later. They'd stayed in a town in the Black Hills the previous night, and were driving to the mountain after an early breakfast.

"That's it!" announced Tom. "That's Crazy Horse mountain. Wow! It is golden. We saw pictures of it that same color."

His mother added, "The morning sun certainly is spotlighting it. Curious none of the other mountains around here stand out like that."

"It's one big mountain," said Mr. Whitney in amazement. "We still must be five or six miles away from it, and look how it dominates the horizon. It must be something to see from the air. I'll bet you can see it for fifty miles—especially on a still morning like this without a cloud in the sky."

"Where is Crazy Horse?" asked Carole, looking at the mountain, "I don't see the Indian."

"Crazy Horse isn't finished yet, dear," said her mother.

"You mean we don't get to see it, then?" said the little girl in disappointment.

"We'll be able to see it in progress. That's what's happening right now. It's being carved," explained her father. "Carole, I think we'll be able to explain it to you better when we get there."

"Dad, do you think we'll meet any real Indians?" asked Tom in an excited voice. "That would be neat."

"I don't know, son. Maybe. We'll be there in a few minutes, and you'll find out then. Carole, before we arrive, let's play our game to see if you can find where we are on the map."

A few minutes later they left the main highway and drove across the Charles Anthony Morss Bridge to Crazy Horse and onto the Avenue of the Chiefs.

"Well, we're almost there, Tom. Remember, I want you on your very best behavior today."

"I will be, Dad."

They were passing a large green and white sign that read:

At the crest of a small hill they stopped at a little white ticket booth. A young lady with a bright smile welcomed them to Crazy Horse. When Tom's father gave his name, she said, "Oh, we've been expecting you. You're to go right on in. I'll call and tell them you're on the way."

"We'd like to pay the admission fee," said Mr. Whitney.

"Oh, no. I'd get in trouble! You're guests of the sculptor. Please just drive right in."

She insisted, so they drove down the Avenue of the Chiefs through a deep valley. Mrs. Whitney said, "After all those miles driving across the dry prairies, these green hills are like an oasis. I don't think I've ever seen so many trees."

"I can't get over the size of that mountain. It looks twice as large from here," observed Mr. Whitney as they came to the crest of another hill and into a large parking lot.

Tom said, "I don't think I'd want to work on any mountain that high. You'd have to be a mountain climber."

"It's not so gold now," said Carole. "It's changing color."

"I suppose that's because the sun is getting a little higher now," said her father.

As they got out of the station wagon, a small lady with a warm smile approached them. "You must be the Whitneys. I'm Mrs. Ziolkowski. Welcome to Crazy Horse. We've been looking forward to having you here. Please call me Ruth. Everyone does."

She wore a robin's egg blue smock over a simple housedress. A pink band held her brown hair—arranged in a small bun—back from her face. She had on white moccasins which caught Carole's interest.

"I'm Jim Whitney. We're delighted to be here. This is my wife, Mary, our daughter, Carole, and this is Tom."

"We've enjoyed your letters, Tom. We appreciate the special interest your class has taken in Crazy Horse. We really do." Her voice was very gentle, and her nose wrinkled when she smiled. Tom blushed a bit as they shook hands. She added, "It's going to be fun having you for the day. Are you sure the rest of you won't change your minds and stay at least for lunch?"

Mr. Whitney said, "Thank you very much, but as we said on the phone, our friends in the area are expecting us. After we've looked around, we'll go to their house, and come back for Tom this evening."

"Well, if you insist. You're more than welcome. In the meantime, let me give you the cook's tour." She held out her hand to Carole, and the little girl took it shyly.

Leaving the parking lot, they entered a wide walkway lined on both sides with works of sculpture standing on high colorful wooden pedestals. Scattered pine trees stood among them. Mrs. Ziolkowski said, "These marble portraits you see here are some of the works my husband carved in the East before he accepted the Indians' invitation to come to the Black Hills. They're Cararra marble from the Italian quarries opened by Michelangelo in 1508."

She stopped in front of the first portrait. "This is the famous Polish pianist and patriot, Ignacy Paderewski. It won the first prize by popular vote at the 1939 New York World's Fair. It's called 'Study of an Immortal.'"

Twice lifesize and positioned slightly above them, the white marble head seemed enormous against the shadowy green pines. A stern countenance gazed out of the marble, framed by a wavy mane of thick hair.

The morning sun highlighted the unusual features—a huge nose, wide, deep-set eyes narrowed to slits below thick, craggy eyebrows, firmly pressed lips, a downturned mouth accented by a short, heavy mustache and goatee above a determined jaw.

"He's frightening!" exclaimed Carole with a little shudder.

"That's a face you wouldn't forget," added her father.

"He was a very intense man," said Mrs. Ziolkowski. "He was a tremendous orator and statesman who wrote the first 13 articles of the Polish Constitution. He also was a world-renowned concert artist, of course. I believe he was the first pianist ever to earn one million dollars a year with his hands.

"This work was the overwhelming popular favorite at the World's Fair. The contest was called: 'I may not know much about art, but I know what I like.' Korczak enjoyed that because he's never had much time for art critics. He likes to put his faith in the public, as he has with Crazy Horse. He says J. Q. Public is the

KORCZAK ©

PADEREWSKI
1,200 pds. Carrara Marble   1935
First Sculptural Award
New York World's Fair—1939
Crazy Horse Memorial

final critic, the one that counts. People loved this Paderewski. They still do."

"It's a very powerful study," observed Mrs. Whitney. "You can feel the magnetism of the man. His strength emerges from the stone. No wonder it took the prize. I wonder what he's thinking about. He seems to be gazing past us. Perhaps he's trying to look into the future."

"What does it weigh?" asked Tom.

"Twelve hundred pounds," said the sculptor's wife. "Korczak carved it in five and one-half days."

"What?" exclaimed Mr. Whitney. "Five and one-half days!"

"Yes, but Korczak says they were 26 hour days . . . ."

The white marble glistened with a soft sheen. Studying the jagged scar where the nose was broken, Mrs. Whitney said sadly, "We read about the vandalism of these pieces of sculpture. What a tragic thing to happen to a man's work."

"What happened to it?" asked Carole, still holding Mrs. Ziolkowski's hand. "Why is his nose broken?"

"Someone attacked it with a hammer," replied her mother. "It's hard to believe anyone could do such a horrible thing."

"No one can understand the senseless destruction of beauty," said Mrs. Ziolkowski coldly. She sighed, and continued along the portrait-lined walkway.

They strolled past Rumanian conductor-pianist Georges Enesco, his large hand in midair conducting a symphony, his delicate aesthetic head cocked to one side, listening to the soaring music,

. . . past Connecticut Governor Wilbur Cross, founder of the *Yale Review,* cloaked in academic robe, holding pen in hand, his round face smiling kindly out of the stone, his eyes twinkling,

. . . past German pianist Artur Schnabel, his craggy features distorted in creative agony, performing a Beethoven sonata.

Tom's father broke the silence, his voice brittle. "I get very angry looking at the senseless disfigurement of these beautiful works."

Ruth said, "Eight works were damaged. Korczak said at the time if they'd have broken every bone in his body, they couldn't have hurt him more. He's faced many hardships out here, but this vandalism of his scuplture was the most shocking and painful. He's never used this entryway since."

Concentrating on the passionate Enesco face, Mrs. Whitney said, "You can see beyond the scars. Each of these portraits has a strong personality."

"Yes. Many people say that," said the sculptor's wife.

They walked on. A gentle breeze stirred the pines and a scattering of needles crunched beneath their feet. Birds were singing.

"I don't believe I've ever walked through an outdoor sculpture gallery like this. That blue sky makes a wonderful ceiling," said Mrs. Whitney. "This seems very European. Old world."

KORCZAK ©

GEORGES ENESCO
Violinist and Composer
Crestola Marble   1937-38
Rumanian Pavilian
New York World's Fair—1939
Crazy Horse Memorial

KORCZAK ©

WILBUR LUCIUS CROSS, Ph.D., L.L.D.
Governor of Connecticut 1930-38
Crestola Marble   1938
Connecticut Building
New York's World's Fair—1939
Crazy Horse Memorial

ARTUR SCHNABEL
Pianist
Serravezza Marble   1936
Crazy Horse Memorial

Mrs. Ziolkowski stopped in front of another portrait, and her smile returned. "This is Judge Frederick Pickering Cabot. In many ways Korczak's story really begins with Judge Cabot."

A large Romanesque head balanced atop a rectangular block of marble. Although the features were heavy, the jaw very square and the expression rather reserved, a friendly face with a certain warmth looked down at them. It had a look of perpetual youth, and the judge seemed to be listening, inquiring with his eyes.

Mrs. Ziolkowski explained, "Korczak was born in Boston of Polish parents who were killed in a boating accident when he was one year old, so he never knew them. If he could have picked another father, it would have been this remarkable man. Judge Cabot presided over the Boston Juvenile Court, which had jurisdiction over Korczak."

Tom frowned. "Did he get into trouble?"

Ruth smiled. "No, he didn't do anything wrong. Let me try to explain it. You see, when his parents were killed, Korczak was orphaned. He didn't have any other relatives. So, he was sent to live in an orphanage, a home for destitute children. Judge Cabot's court looked after the welfare of children like that, who were all alone in the world."

"An orphanage sounds awful," said Carole, making a face.

"It was quite bad. Then, he was sent to live in a series of foster homes. When he was your age, Tom, he lived with an Irish prizefighter and his wife. He was with them 12 years from age 4 to 16. The wife was so cruel to the boy, he left when he was 16. He still was in school, so he took a variety of odd jobs to work his way through Rindge Technical School in Cambridge, Massachusetts. But, since he still wasn't an adult, he had to report to Judge Cabot. The judge was his guardian, really.

"When Korczak graduated, he got a job as an apprentice in the patternmaking shop of Bethlehem Steel on the tough Boston waterfront. In his spare time, he experimented in that shop, and it was Judge Cabot who recognized the boy had a great gift for working with wood. When we go inside, I'll show you some of the beautiful things he made as a teenager."

"He really began life with the cards stacked against him, didn't he?" noted Mr. Whitney.

"Things began to change when Judge Cabot befriended him. He did everything he could to encourage Korczak to develop his talents. He would invite Korczak into his home. He and his sister, Amy Cabot, would take Korczak with them to the Boston Symphony and many other activities. They introduced him to wonderful people in the fields of art, music, sculpture and literature. As an orphan growing up in foster homes, he'd never been exposed to cultural events."

"Was Judge Cabot sort of like a teacher to him?" asked Tom.

"Well, yes, Tom. A great teacher, but much more," said Ruth. "He was known as the 'children's judge' because he took such a great, personal interest in helping young people who didn't have anyone else. He became quite famous in his field. He founded the Judge Baker Guidance Center in Boston; he was the first president of the Boston Symphony; and he was on the Board of Directors of the

15

MEMORIAL TO
JUDGE FREDERICK PICKERING CABOT
Created by Korczak   1935
Sculptor, Architect and Engineer
Symphony Hall
Boston, Massachusettes

Perkins Institute for the Blind, Wentworth Institute, Radcliffe, Harvard, the Boston Museum of Fine Arts and many, many more boards of directors for very worthy causes.

"When Judge Cabot died, Korczak made a marble portrait of him. It was his first work in stone. He didn't have any sculpting tools, so he used an old coal chisel and a crude hammer. He didn't even make a clay model, just created the portrait right in the stone. That's the classical way the old masters like Leonardo da Vinci and Michelangelo worked. Most of Korczak's works are done like that. You can't afford to make a mistake when you do it that way."

"But, who taught him how to do it?" Tom asked.

"It was a natural gift. He taught himself how to use it. From a very early age he was a great reader, but Korczak never had a master and never took one lesson in art or sculpture or engineering."

"He's self-taught! That's amazing," said Tom's father.

Ruth added, "Self-taught, but guided and encouraged at a very formative age by Judge Cabot. He believed in the boy and introduced whole new worlds to him. Notice the block base on which the portrait is standing. That cut across it similar to an 'L' is like the keystone of the foundation of a building. It's symbolic that Judge Cabot was a keystone in the lives of so many young people. Later, Korczak made two other portraits of him. Judge Cabot's cultural and intellectual influence on Korczak was so profound and far-reaching, you see, Judge Cabot is where the Crazy Horse story really begins."

They walked on into the visitor center.

"There's Crazy Horse," exclaimed Carole, letting go of Ruth's hand.

"Wow!" said Tom. The two youngsters rushed across a wide covered porch to a giant model of Crazy Horse astride his rearing pony. It stood on an open veranda where it gleamed a brilliant white in the morning sun against a backdrop of the dark trees, the blue sky and the mountain looming in the distance.

"This is Korczak's large plaster model for the mountain carving," explained Mrs. Ziolkowski, as she and the Whitneys approached the big model. "The mountain, which is being carved in the round, will look just like this model when it's finished."

"It's very dramatic," said Mr. Whitney. "How large is it?"

"It's 18½ feet tall on a scale of 1/34th the size of the mountain carving. Korczak made it one winter, and almost froze his hands working in the wet plaster."

"That horse really looks mad," said Tom, studying the rearing head.

"The horse's head will be 22 stories high when it's finished."

Photograph of the 563-foot high Crazy Horse mountain carving in progress with approximately seven million, two hundred thousand tons of granite removed. Inserted as a point of reference is Korczak's large scale model for the sculpture-in-the-round. The 18½-foot high plaster model was created by Korczak in 1965 on a scale of 1/34th the size of the mountain carving.

17

"What is Crazy Horse pointing at?" asked Carole. The Indian's left arm was thrust out over the horse's head. His finger pointed firmly to the east.

"To his lands where his dead lie buried . . ." answered Mrs. Ziolkowski. She paused for a moment to smile for a little old lady with a camera who had moved in to sneak a picture of Ruth. Tom noticed a crowd had started to gather around them as visitors recognized the sculptor's wife. Several more cameras clicked.

"I was going to tell you about the overall project," said Ruth turning back to the Whitneys, "but since we've drawn quite a crowd, I may as well do a porch lecture while I'm out here. We have a slide program in our theater to orient visitors about the project, but for the first 30 years we gave regular lectures out here."

Turning back to the onlookers, she said, "If you folks would all like to gather around that glass case right over there, I'd be happy to tell you a little more about Crazy Horse."

With the Whitneys she walked over to the case. It contained an architectural model of what looked like a small town. Scores of miniature buildings and roads spread out in front of a little model of Crazy Horse. Tiny trees covered the rolling hills and valleys. There was a long airfield at one end of the model. The entrance highway ran beneath it.

"What you see here is an architectural model of what Crazy Horse will look like one day in the future," Mrs. Ziolkowski told the group. "To understand it, you must realize Crazy Horse is much more than a mountain carving.

"When Korczak accepted the Indians' invitation to carve the mountain to their great chief, he promised them it would be a non-profit humanitarian project to benefit the Indian people. So, Crazy Horse has not one but three major goals: the mountain carving, the Indian Museum of North America and the University and Medical Training Center for the North American Indian.

"It all will be financed by the interested public, by people just like you who want to come here. All the revenue comes from the admission fee, contributions and a portion of the souvenir sales. No tax dollars ever will be involved. We operate on a day-to-day, pay-as-you-go basis."

Mrs. Whitney lifted Carole up so she could get a better look at the architectural model. On it, Ruth pointed out the location of the present visitor complex. "Where you're standing right now is almost one mile away from the mountain. When the heavy blasting is finished, the buildings you see on this architectural model will rise between here and the mountain.

"The Museum will be very unusual. It is this round building you see on the model near the base of the mountain. Architecturally, it will be a hogan, a circular building with a large round opening in the center of the roof. It's a Southwest Indian design, looking a little like a giant igloo. The opening will let in the sun and the elements. All the artifacts will be safely housed under glass. The Museum will be built from the stone blasted off the mountain, as will many of these other buildings for the University and Medical Training Center."

Someone asked, "Will we be able to go around to the other side of the mountain? It looks like that on this model."

"Yes, indeed," said Ruth, "The road you see leading around to the other side of the mountain will take visitors back there because Crazy Horse is being sculpted in the round. Many people don't realize that."

"Can we go back there now?" came another voice from the crowd.

"No. Not now. It's too dangerous with the ongoing blasting on the mountain. It isn't safe now. This is for the future. You'll notice the large reflecting pool around the base of the mountain. That will be a man-made lake fed from the many natural springs around the mountain. People are surprised to learn that every lake in the Black Hills is man made. The lake won't come until the work on the mountain is nearly completed, in the future.

"Most of the buildings you see on this architectural model also will come later, but the cultural and educational phases of the project are underway now. The Indian Museum now is housed in this complex. And, Korczak has established a series of Indian scholarships which have launched the educational phase, in a modest way.

"Until it is finished, of course, the mountain carving will continue to be the number one priority. Korczak has blasted off more than seven million tons so far, blocking out the rough form of Crazy Horse and his pony.

"If you'll compare the mountain with the big model on the veranda, you'll see against the sky the rough outline of the Indian's 90-foot-high head, the long flat area above his 263-foot-long arm, the opening under the arm, which one day will be able to house a 10-story building, and the rough form of the horse's head, which is 219 feet high. The horse's head is so big a five-room house would fit inside its nostril and his left eye will be two stories high. Korczak and the boys are working on that right now. You can see them with the naked eye, but the binoculars on the veranda will bring the mountain much closer. Remember, it's nearly one mile away from you."

Mrs. Ziolkowski paused, smiling at the large crowd ringing the architectural model. "I know you'll have many questions, but if you'd all care to step into our theater, I think most of them will be answered. I see they're just ready to announce the next slide program. Please have a nice visit."

As the slide program was announced, most of the onlookers left for the theater.

As Ruth led the Whitney family toward the Museum, Mrs. Whitney kidded her, "I suspect you might have given that interesting lecture a time or two before."

"Oh, my, yes. For years I did them all. In the beginning there wasn't any money for staff, so I worked alone here with the visitors while Korczak worked alone up on the mountain. This was all open then, and I'd get quite a suntan. Even the inside of my lips would be sunburned by the end of the summer. The story is much easier to tell now because Korczak's great progress on the mountain speaks for itself.

"Before we step into the Museum, I'd like to point out Korczak's portrait of Gutzon Borglum, who carved Mt. Rushmore here in the Black Hills. Korczak assisted him briefly, and he holds Mr. Borglum in great esteem. His portrait has a place of honor here."

21

GUTZON BORGLUM
Sculptor of Mt. Rushmore
Bas Relief Study   Plaster   1962
Crazy Horse Memorial

CHAPTER 3

THE STORY OF THE DRUM

Oh, how beautiful!" exclaimed Mrs. Whitney as they stepped into the Indian Museum.

It was a very long, two and one-half story hall, the walls, ceiling and floor of which were rich natural pine. It was a lustrous reddish-brown, enhanced by natural light from long windows at the high ceiling that ran the full length of the Museum. There was a sanctuary hush in the big room.

On all four walls and in glass cases also running the length of the room were colorful Indian artifacts—headdresses with long trails of eagle feathers, delicate beaded buckskin dresses and vests with intricate geometric and floral patterns, blankets, woven baskets, pipes, bows and arrows and much more.

"It's like a church," whispered Carole.

"Many people feel that," said Mrs. Ziolkowski. "We notice they speak very softly or even whisper in here. I do it myself."

Tom's father was studying one of several quotation boards on the walls. They had distinctive Old English lettering in shiny gold leaf. He read aloud:

> They made us many promises,
> more than I can remember—
> they never kept but one:
> They promised to take our land,
> and they took it.
> —Red Cloud

"That's quite an indictment," said Mr. Whitney.

"These quotations, in part, illustrate that American Indians are a very sensitive and proud people. Korczak picked these eloquent quotations. They say a great deal about the Indian."

The Indian Museum of North America

She was interrupted by Tom, whose eyes had grown large.

He whispered loudly to his father, "Dad. Look! There's an Indian!"

"Tom," said his father sharply, "don't interrupt, and what have I told you about pointing at people?" But, Tom definitely was pointing to a man at the end of the museum at whom the family was gazing. He was talking with a group of people.

A big man with broad shoulders, the object of Tom's attention, excused himself and came toward them. He moved quietly with a rather slow, rolling gate. He was about 60 years old, and was dressed in modern clothing, which included a beautifully beaded vest. His face and hands were a ruddy brown, and he had quick dark eyes that studied as he approached.

His long face was dominated by a heavy nose, high forehead and large ears. They were accented because his greying hair was pulled tightly back into a small pony tail with two downy bird feathers tied in it at a rakish angle with a piece of buckskin. His hair glistened in the Museum's natural light.

"This is George Small," said Mrs. Ziolkowski, introducing everyone. "We're happy to have Mr. Small and his wife here to tell our visitors about the Indian artifacts in this room. He'll answer any questions you might have."

"That's a very pretty dress you're wearing, young lady," he said to Carole, who looked shyly up at him. He spoke very softly and deliberately and had a slight accent the Whitneys had not heard before.

Tom stared intently at Mr. Small, who seemed to be reading the boy's mind. "I'll bet you're wondering about me," said the big man. Tom blushed. "I talk with lots of young fellows like you. I imagine you'd like to know about those bows and arrows over there. I learned to use them when I grew up on the Standing Rock Reservation on the North Dakota-South Dakota border. My parents were full-blooded Lakota Indians," Mr. Small said proudly.

Tom said cautiously, "I really would like to hear about the bows and arrows."

"I'll be glad to tell you."

Ruth said, "I think we interrupted Mr. Small's tour. I see he was talking with that group of people."

"Yes. I should get back to them," he said. "I'll join you later to answer your questions. There are over 50 tribes represented here, and really, these beautiful artifacts speak for themselves. If you examine them closely, you'll be able to learn a great deal about Indian culture. The best thing visitors can do here is use their eyes. I'll join you in just a little while."

As he returned to the other group, Mrs. Ziolkowski said, "While he finishes, let me point out something I think will interest you all. It will tell you a lot about Indian symbolism."

She walked to the end of the museum where a very large, colorful Indian drum stood on a high stand. With the help of Tom's father, she put the drum on the floor. It was almost as tall as Carole, who patted it gently with her hand. It made a soft "Boom, boom."

"Carole, don't touch the drum," said her mother quickly.

"Oh, that's all right," said Ruth. "I don't imagine you've ever seen a drum like that, have you, Carole and Tom?"

"No," said Tom, wide-eyed. "Is it a real Indian drum? What are all those pictures and designs on it?"

"That's the story of the drum," Ruth explained. "It was a gift to Korczak from the Iroquois Indians in the Northeast. That beautiful beadwork there on the wall came with it and tells about the gift. I'll explain the pictures and signs to you:

"The cover of the drum is made of deer skin. Here on the top of the drum is painted the Morning Star. In the center of this star is a painting of the mountain as it will look when the Memorial is finished. Above the star is a spirit picture showing the Spirit of Crazy Horse looking down on the monument with approval. Korczak's Indian name is Brave Wolf, given to him by the Sioux Indians here in South Dakota. So, the top of the drum shows the Spirit of Crazy Horse looking down with favor on Brave Wolf's work below.

"Around the sides of the drum, here, are painted tracks of the grizzly bear, which fears nothing. He is very brave and nothing can turn him aside. The Iroquois Indians said, 'Brave Wolf, we wish you to continue to have the courage of the grizzly bear, that you will, in spite of all obstacles that may attempt to stop you, be like the grizzly bear—going ahead with this project—that you will not turn aside until you have completed it.'

"Here, along the bottom of the drum are the tracks of the buffalo, which mean plenty. The Iroquois said this means: 'Brave Wolf, we wish that you will have plenty of food, shelter and clothing for yourself, your wife and your 10 children while you are working on this project, and that interested people will see that you have plenty of the necessary money to finance your work to complete this memorial to Indians.'

"This other set of tracks around the top and bottom of the drum are the tracks of the raccoon. The Iroquois said: 'This means—the raccoon is an animal who goes about both at night and in the day. Brave Wolf, may you never tire, day or night, until you have seen this project through—completed.'

"Around the top and bottom or cylinder of the drum this step-like design you see means the Tree of Peace. The Indians said: 'This represents the Great Peace Law of the Iroquois Confederacy, the Ever Growing Tree planted by Deganewida, founder of the Iroquois Confederacy, in the days before the coming of the White Man to this, our land. The Iroquois or Six Nations Indians are aware of this great work you are doing, Brave Wolf, this project to honor all Indians across this Great Island. They are grateful and appreciative, Brave Wolf, for your good heart.'"

Tom and Carole now were sitting on the floor, intently listening to Mrs. Ziolkowski tell the story of the big drum. They seemed unaware that another large crowd had gathered behind them.

Ruth tells the story of the drum to Tom and Carole

26

Tom said, "The drum is telling a story."

"Yes," said Ruth, "and there's more. These figures of Indians painted on the sides of the drum represent the four great Indian families who live in North America. This is how the Iroquois explain the meaning of these four scenes: 'The Indians of the Plains, of the Northwest Coast, of the desert and of the forest thank and honor you, Brave Wolf, for what you are trying to do for Indian Peoples, causing honor, friendship and respect for them among the peoples of the world.'

"Now, you see an animal painted under each of the four scenes of the four Indian families. Among the Iroquois people these four animals represent the four winds. This is the Great Bear, who lives in the northern sky, the little fawn lives in the southern sky, the great moose lives in the eastern sky, and the fierce mountain lion lives in the western sky."

"The Iroquois who gave this drum to Korczak say the symbols of the four winds mean this: 'We have heard that certain white men in "high places" have said to you, "Why do you honor Indian People? They will not appreciate what you are doing for them." This is not true, Brave Wolf! Indians of the North, the South, the East and the West, appreciate and are grateful for the great work you are doing for Indian Peoples, Brave Wolf. They are an appreciative people . . . especially those who follow the Old Way, the Indian Way.'

"The Indians who presented this drum added, 'It is a gift to you two friends, Brave Wolf and your good wife and helper, Ruth, from the Long House People, the Kanonsionni—the Mohawks—the Oneidas—the Onondagas—Cayugas—the Tuscaroras and the Senecas—We honor you, Brave Wolf, for your courage and for your good heart. May Sakoiatison, Our Creator, cause the sun to shine strong in your heart and may He cause your lodge to be filled with plenty of good things.' "

Mrs. Ziolkowski paused, smiling at the two youngsters sitting on the floor beside the big drum. "And, that's the story the Iroquois painted on this drum. You see, it's a most unusual drum, very special."

"I like the name Brave Wolf," said Carole.

"It's sure easier to pronounce," said Tom. He wished he hadn't said it when he heard his father clear his throat. But, there was laughter from several of the people who had come to hear Ruth tell the story of the drum. Tom blushed violently.

As they walked toward the exit, Mrs. Whitney said, "There are so many interesting things in this beautiful museum, we'll want to spend some more time here. But, we don't want to keep you. With all these visitors, you must have a million things to do."

Ruth smiled. "Things do get a bit hectic. My daughters are a great help to me, though. I probably should check in with them to see what crisis has arisen. Let me just show you the 'log cabin' studio-home, and then I'll let you look around at your own pace."

"That's what I want to see," said Tom excitedly. "The log cabin."

POLISH EAGLE
Tennessee Marble   1947
Size: 24 inches
Crazy Horse Memorial

CHAPTER 4

THE LOG CABIN

N ow you're entering the original studio-home," said Mrs. Ziolkowki. They had come back across the crowded veranda and covered porch, and were entering a spacious room also built completely of wood.

The light tan knotty pine walls and ceiling had a seasoned look. The floor was inlaid oak, polished to a deep luster. The room seemed to glow with soft indirect light from a wide northern skylight running the width of the room. The natural wood and light gave a cozy warmth to the big room, which was crowded with sculpture, paintings, antiques and unusual furnishings. The focal point was an ebony concert grand piano, which glistened like polished marble.

"Where's the log cabin?" asked Tom.

Ruth smiled. "This is the log cabin. You're standing in it. See the big log beams running across the ceiling? The outside walls of this room are made from logs just like that, notched to fit on top of one another. You can see them outside that other door."

Tom looked puzzled. "I never thought a log cabin looked like this."

"I don't think this is your average log cabin," remarked Mr. Whitney, studying the beams. "How long are those logs?"

"Some are 70 feet," Ruth replied. "They were cut from this property. This was all wilderness when Korczak arrived the spring of 1947. There were no roads, water or electricity. So, before he could begin the mountain carving, he had to build a place to live."

"I read he lived in a tent," said Tom.

"Yes. The first seven months. He had only $174 left to his name when he arrived here to start this project, so he had to live in a tent while he built this log home."

"It really smells good in here," Carole said.

"That's lunch in the oven. Our kitchen is just on the other side of that little doorway there."

"You live right here?" asked Mrs. Whitney.

"Yes. We always have. Korczak and I were married in this room. This was Korczak's studio and our home the first few years. We heated it with that big fireplace there. Then, as more and more visitors started arriving and as the family grew, Korczak added a room or two every year. He built a sawmill here to provide all the lumber. Today there are about 61 rooms. We sort of grew like Topsy. I'm reminded of it every time it rains hard. There's always a leak at some seam where a newer roof was attached to an older roof. We have to get out all the pots and pans to catch the drips."

"Like at home when Daddy didn't fix the roof after the hailstorm?" asked Carole.

Her father frowned at her, and she bit her lip. Before he could say anything, resonant chimes rang out from a tall clock standing on the floor beside the grand piano.

"I don't think this is your average log cabin," said Mr. Whitney.

KORCZAK ©

GRANDFATHER'S CLOCK
Fifty-five pieces of Santa Domingo Mahogany designed
and carved by Korczak at age 18

Dimensions:
   Height: 8 ft. 2½ in.
   Width: 22½ in.
   Depth: 15½ in.

Movement:
   Westminster Big Ben Chimes
   (last ever made at the
   Waltham, Mass. Clock Co.)

FIGHTING STALLIONS
Single block of African Mahogany   1940
Height: 18 inches
Crazy Horse Memorial

Mrs. Whitney said, "That grandfather's clock is exquisite."

"It's a beauty," echoed her husband. The stately clock was a glossy reddish mahogany accented by a dark grain weaving through the rich wood. Carole went over to listen to the tick tock and watch the big brass pendulum swing.

"Korczak made this clock when he was 18 working in the patternmaking shop on the Boston waterfront that I told you about earlier. This clock has 55 separate pieces, all hand carved. It's Santa Domingo mahogany from pieces of fine wood that Korczak bought in Boston. The plans for it are there on the wall.

"In the patternmaking shop he made several elaborate pieces of furniture, experimenting and teaching himself to work with wood. Judge Cabot loved this clock. He'd come to Korczak's little apartment and watch Korczak take it all apart and put the 55 pieces back together again."

"Craftsmanship like that is almost a lost art these days," said Mr. Whitney.

The sculptor's wife nodded. "He gave this clock away when he was a young man, but we're very happy it has come back to us now. I think it belongs here."

"Mommy, look at the horses fighting," said Carole. "They're biting and kicking each other." She was standing on her tiptoes with Tom beside the grand piano on which stood a wood sculpture of two horses. They were rearing up on their back legs striking out at one another with their front legs. Their ears were laid back, their teeth bared, and their blood vessels and muscles bulging in the strain of mortal combat.

"They look very angry indeed," said Mrs. Whitney, lifting the little girl to get a better view of the horses.

"Those are Korczak's famous *Fighting Stallions*," said Mrs. Ziolkowski.

"They're both balanced on the one horse's tail," marveled Mr. Whitney.

"He carved them free standing from a single piece of African mahogany. Notice how he's used the grain of the wood, and they are partially carved against the grain, which is very difficult to accomplish without shattering the wood."

"Did he make these as a teenager, too?" asked Mr. Whitney.

"No. These were carved when he was in his late 20's. Many people feel they are a masterpiece."

"I can easily see why they might think that," he said. "Did he do any larger works before starting the mountain?"

"His *Noah Webster* statue in West Hartford, Connecticut is 13 and one-half feet tall. It would have been taller, but he reduced it several inches so it would not be taller than Michelangelo's *David*. It's Tennessee marble, a lovely stone with a pink tone. He gave it as a gift to West Hartford, where Korczak lived during the 1930's. It was also Noah Webster's birthplace, but there was no memorial to him there or anywhere. You'll see several pictures of it in the next room. The *Polish Eagle* you saw earlier is carved from a piece of marble taken from a shoulder cut for the *Noah Webster* statue.

"Korczak wanted to honor Noah because his dictionary became the common denominator for our language in this country. So, he made that heroic statue, and gave it away. He has given away many of his works just as all the effort—his life really—that he is putting into Crazy Horse is so that the Indian people will benefit from the project."

33

Sculptor Korczak Ziolkowski in 1942 seated by the 33 ton, 14½ ft. tall block of Tennessee marble from which he carved the *Noah Webster* statue.

KORCZAK ©

NOAH WEBSTER STATUE
Tennessee Marble   1942-43
Height: 13 ft. 6 in.
Weight: 22 tons
Town Hall Lawn
West Hartford, Connecticut

"This is a wonderful room," said Mrs. Whitney. "Are these paintings of your husband?"

"Yes. This one was painted when he was only 23 years old. It was painted by Jacob Binder. This one across the room from it was painted 50 years later. They make an interesting contrast."

"He sure has changed," Tom said.

"It has to be very hard work carving a mountain," noted his father.

Mrs. Whitney stood silently gazing around at the sculpture-filled room. Finally she said, "Your husband must be a very unusual man. I certainly never expected to discover an island of fine art on a mountaintop in the middle of the Black Hills. It's another world."

Mrs. Ziolkowski smiled. "That's a very astute observation. The world of art, sculpture and music he knew and loved in the East he gave up to accept the Indians' invitation to carve Crazy Horse. It's a very different world out here, but he came willingly. He didn't anticipate the degree of hardship he'd face here, but he'd be the first to say there have been many rewards, too. He has no regrets.

"The mountain carving has become his life, and that's the way he wanted it. He always has said the mountain comes first. The children and I understand that. Michelangelo said a man could not have his art and his mistress at the same time. I think Korczak has proved him wrong. He has his work and his wife and family, although the work comes first. We know that.

"And, speaking of family, I'd better check that roast or we'll be having a crisp lunch, and I'll be in the doghouse."

"Thank you so much for taking the time to show us around," said Mrs. Whitney.

"Be sure not to miss Korczak's workshop through that door. It's open to the public. I think Tom and Carole will enjoy the beautiful stagecoach on display there. It's a Concord coach authentically restored by one of our daughters, Monique. You'll find many more of Korczak's sculptures there as well. Are you sure you won't stay for lunch? You're more than welcome."

"Thank you, no. We'll go on to visit our friends. Tom will stay for the afternoon. It's Tom's big day."

KORCZAK ©

BLANCHE YURKA
Portrait of an Actress
Crestola Marble   1937
Life Size
Crazy Horse Memorial

HEAD OF A HORSE
Honduras Mahogany   1940
Life Size   Carved in nine days
Crazy Horse Memorial

CHAPTER 5

TOM MEETS KORCZAK

Shortly before noon Tom's parents and sister departed. As he walked back from the parking lot with Mrs. Ziolkowski, the boy wondered what it was like living in the rambling visitor complex open to the public. He didn't know what to expect.

They went through a short entryway bridging the public and the private worlds, and stepped through yet another door. "This is the family dining room," said Ruth, gesturing him to a seat. "It's rather quiet at the moment, but it won't be for long. Korczak and the family will be in for lunch soon. Which reminds me, I'd better check the oven again. Please excuse me for a minute."

Alone for the first time, Tom felt he was peeking backstage. He looked around the rustic room. It was rather small and cheerful, and looked very lived in. It was all wood, like the other rooms he had seen. There was a wonderful aroma coming from the kitchen.

Lots of natural light came from a big north window, which gave a full view of the mountain carving. Two large lamps with bright red glass shades hung above the long table that looked like an oversize work bench. Tom thought about a dozen people could sit around it.

There were only three chairs. At the head of the table there was a heavy wooden chair with big arms and a high back. Next to it was a rocking chair, and across from it one plain kitchen chair. A wide bench with a high back ran all along one side and around the other end of the long table. That's where Tom was sitting. The other side of the long table had no chairs at all.

He could barely hear the murmur of the visitors in the public part of the house. As he listened, he heard a door open, and Korczak entered.

Tom recognized him immediately from TV. He was a tall man with a rugged build. His big beard was bushier and greyer than Tom expected. A long mustache flowed down and disappeared in the beard.

"Hello," said Korczak, striding across the room. "You must be Tom Whitney."

"Yes, sir," said Tom, jumping up as Ruth returned to introduce them formally.

She added, "This is the young man who wrote such nice letters to you."

Korczak greets his young visitor

Tom wanted to study the large firm hand shaking his. He knew that hand had made beautiful sculpture, but he couldn't take his eyes off the holes in

40

Korczak's hat. It wasn't quite a cowboy hat, but it looked like it had seen a lot of trails. The front brim looked like something had taken a large bite out of it, and there was another big nick in the top. In addition to having several other small tears, it was grease-spotted and quite dirty. It had been light tan, and the hat seemed to have a personality of its own.

Smiling down at him, Korczak said, "How nice you could come to visit us. I hope you're staying for lunch with the family."

"He certainly is, but I couldn't persuade his family to stay. They have some friends in the area they've gone off to visit. Mr. Whitney said this was Tom's day. He's representing his class, you remember."

"Say, that's some class. Well, I'm sorry your family couldn't stay, but you and I will have a nice time. Go ahead, walk the plank! That's what my children call it. Slide around on that bench to that chair beside mine. We couldn't find a table big enough for this family, so I built this one. I built this whole room. It's the nerve center of this project. I built mother a beautiful office, but she won't use it. No, she has to do everything on the dining room table. This is her office!"

Although it was rather warm, Korczak was wearing over his work clothes a buckskin jacket. It had fringe on it, and made him look like a frontiersman. Ruth was helping him out of it. As she took his hat, he told Tom, "This old hat is a good friend of mine. We've been through a lot together. This jacket, too. That's my own blood there on the lapel. I got that when I tipped over a jeep on the other side of the mountain.

"You have to wear a jacket up there. You perspire and get damp working that big Cat; then, if you don't have protection from the wind on the mountain, you catch cold. It's always windy up there, even if it's calm down here."

Tom wanted to ask him about the holes in the hat, but thought better of it. Korczak must have been reading his mind. "I got those holes from flying rocks. We have some pretty big blasts up there." The sculptor chuckled, and added, "Besides, I need a hat these days because I have a lot more hair on my chin than I have left on the top of my head."

Korczak had a big voice that filled the room. The boy was surprised he had an accent like Tom's uncle who lived in Massachusetts. The sculptor's face and hands were weatherbeaten, and his penetrating eyes were a cold blue.

"There. That's better," said Korczak, sitting down in the big chair with the arms. "That was a good morning we had on the mountain. I got quite a bit of rock pushed off." He picked up a pair of old black binoculars, and studied the mountain through the big window.

"You can work for months up there, and still you can't see much change from down here. People just don't realize the size of that mountain." He sighed, and put the binoculars back on the hook beside his chair.

"I watched you bulldozing from out front this morning," said Tom. "We looked through the binoculars on the veranda."

"That bulldozer looks pretty small from down here. Now, please, you must call me Korczak. That's all I use anymore. Nobody can pronounce my last name anyway. It's so long, and I'm getting too old to write it all out. So, I just sign Korczak. It saves a lot of time, and that's the most important thing!" He winked at

Tom, whose nervousness had disappeared. Korczak's fatherly manner had put him at ease.

The sculptor asked about Tom's family and the trip to South Dakota. While Tom answered, Korczak lit a long cigar. The cloud of grey smoke made Tom's nose tickle.

"So your father's a dentist. We could use a dentist at Crazy Horse with all the children. Mother, where are they? What you're cooking smells very good."

As if in answer, the screendoor opened, and two young men came in. They were in their mid 20's, deeply suntanned and very muscular. Each one walked over and kissed Korczak on his forehead.

"These are my sons, Adam and Casimir," said Korczak. "This is Tom Whitney. I told you he'd be visiting us today."

The sons said hello, and each leaned over the table to shake hands with the intent young visitor.

"What took you so long?" asked Korczak. "Tom and I are starving."

"That was a dirty job up there this morning," said Adam. "It took awhile to get all that dirt off."

"We ate enough dust today so we shouldn't be hungry," said Cas.

"Those boys work very hard—some of the time," said Korczak. "Adam is my right-hand man. He's the hardest worker of all. He's also the milkman now. We only have a few cows left, but he takes care of them. He rounds them up every night, and milks them. That provides all the milk and cream for the family. Then, we butcher in the fall, and that provides some of our meat."

The two boys didn't look much alike. Adam was taller, darker and rather skinny. Cas was stockier, blond.

"Now, Casimir there works very hard when he works, but sometimes he doesn't work. I always say if there are 999 ways to do a thing right and one way to do it wrong, he'll find that one way to do it wrong. He's a genius at it! Yes, sir, that's my Casimir."

"Not everyone can do that," replied Casimir, smiling.

"Thank goodness for that! Ah, here are my two youngest daughters!"

Two attractive girls bounced into the room. Each said, "Hello, Daddy," and gave their father a kiss on the cheek.

"You see, Tom, we're a very lovey-dovey family. This is our daughter, Monique, and this is Marinka, our youngest. They've all graduated from high school now, so I must be getting older."

After Tom was introduced, Monique welcomed him to Crazy Horse. Turning to her father, she said, "I got the eagle almost finished this morning. Want to see it?"

"Sure! Go get it. Bring it in." To Tom he explained, "Monique and Cas, when he has the time, are working on a new gate for out front. It will be very large and be inset with hundreds of brass silhouettes of animals, birds, plants and trees native to the Black Hills. It's going to be almost a textbook.

"Monique is researching all about the birds and animals, then drawing an outline of each. Cas even tries his hand at drawing some of them. She traces the outline on the brass, and Cas cuts them out. They both do the engraving of the details on the anatomy—such as beaks, claws and feathers.

"These birds and animals all have to be alive with action and motion. They are swooping or jumping. The frogs are wonderful. One has his long tongue out catching a big fly! We've had a hard time getting the eagle just right. I'll be interested to see . . . ah, here she is with it!"

Monique held up the 18-inch brass silhouette for her father's inspection. It gleamed as the light reflected off it. There was a long silence as Korczak studied the eagle. In its powerful claws it held a trout. It apparently had just grabbed the fish from the water and was spreading its wings to lift off into the sky. Monique glanced nervously at Cas, who rolled his eyes.

At last Korczak said, "That's something! Now you've got it right. That's quite a piece of work. I can't fault it."

Everybody seemed to relax. Monique and Cas beamed, and the girl explained to Tom how she and her brother created the birds and animals. It sounded very difficult, and Tom said as much.

"Some of these youngsters are quite gifted," said their father. "But, they have to work at it. A gift is one thing. Developing and using it—that's quite another thing. Did you see the stagecoach?"

"Oh, yes, sir. I never saw a real stagecoach before," said Tom.

"Monique and Adam worked to make that so beautiful. You should have seen it when we got it. A wreck. But, Monique spent over a year restoring it authentically. It's carefully researched. We're very proud of that stagecoach. It will be part of an early Americana display we're planning here for the future. Well, here's Joel."

Another young man entered. Like the others, he crossed over and greeted his father with a peck on the top of the head. He was younger, taller and slimmer than the other boys, topped with a bush of very curly blond hair. As he was being introduced as the youngest son, another young woman came in.

Korczak said, "This is my Annie."

"Hello, General," said Anne, coming over to give him a loud kiss on the lips.

Korczak smacked his lips and winked again at Tom. "You'll have to watch out for Annie. She'll steal your heart if you aren't careful."

As she greeted him, Tom blushed and smiled shyly. She had brown wavy hair, wistful hazel eyes and peaches and cream complexion.

"Annie is in charge over in the Indian museum. I hope you had a chance to see that. Did you see everything this morning?" asked Korczak.

"Yes, sir. Your wife showed us all around. It was very interesting," Tom replied.

"Good. Mother, can't we eat now?"

"Yes, dear," she said coming into the dining room carrying a large platter with a big beef roast on it. "You'll carve for us, won't you?"

"Say, look at that," said Korczak. "It's one of ours, isn't it?"

"Yes, from the cow we butchered last winter. I thought you might like this since we have company today."

"This is some of Adam's work, Tom. Adam, why don't you do the carving today? You do such a good job, and Tom and I are having a nice time down here.

43

Why don't one of you boys get up and help your mother with that? It must be heavy. Why do I have to tell you?"

As the roast was being situated for Adam to carve at the end of the long table, another striking young woman came in. She was tall and slender with golden hair that came almost down to her waist. It shimmered as she moved.

"This is our daughter, Jadwiga," he told Tom as she leaned down to kiss her father on the cheek.

He introduced Tom, and she said, "I hope you and your family had an enjoyable visit this morning."

"Jadwiga is named after a queen of Poland, and Casimir, the little rascal, is named after Casimir the Great, a famous king of Poland. My parents were Polish, although they died when I was very young. That lovely girl, Jadwiga, I delivered. She was born on a stormy night, and I guess she was in a hurry. She wouldn't wait for the doctor to get here, so what could I do? I had to deliver her."

"You did?" exclaimed Tom.

"Yup. It was a difficult birth, too. I was pretty nervous, but Mother coached me a little. All the children were born in this house. Whoever thought I'd have a big family like this? I was almost 40 when I came out here from Connecticut, and Mother and I didn't get married for a couple of years after that. Look at us now.

"It's wonderful to have them all here. Three have left, two boys and a girl, but these seven are here. I think that's quite remarkable. The boys work with me up there on the mountain and the girls help their mother run this down here. Yes, I think that's rather unusual."

He puffed the cigar, surveying the family around him. "Casimir is the reason I smoke these cigars. It's his fault. When he was born, I thought it would be sort of nice to give away a cigar or two. So, I bought a box of them. Never had one before. Well, I had to try one myself, and that started me on them. Now I'm hooked. I never smoked a cigarette until the Battle of the Bulge in World War Two. Maybe you've heard of it. None of us thought we'd come out of it, so when someone offered me a cigarette, I took it. What difference did it make? I was 37 then."

Stroking his big beard, Korczak added, "I never planned to have a beard like this either. My oldest daughter Dawn was very ill once. The doctors didn't think she would live. It was touch and go for awhile, but when she opened her eyes in that hospital room, oh, she was so pale and fragile, she looked up at me and said, 'Daddy, would you buy me a red dress?' I said, 'Yes, dear, of course. Is there anything else?' She looked up at me for a long moment, then said, 'Yes, there is one thing. Would you grow a beard for me?' Well, Tom, I went out and bought her a whole outfit in red. And, I've had the beard ever since!"

Adam had finished carving the roast, and the plates were being served. Korczak said, "That's quite a piece of beef Adam has given you, Tom. I hope you have a good appetite. I do."

Tom had begun to feel right at home. He had lots of questions, but sat quietly remembering his dad's reminder to be on his best behavior. His eyes and ears were alert with curiosity about this unusual family. As they ate, he said to Korczak, "This really tastes wonderful. Thank you for inviting me to stay."

Tom joins the big family for lunch

Korczak reached over and patted him on the shoulder. "It's our pleasure, Tom. I was very touched by the letters from your classmates telling of your studies about Crazy Horse. That was quite a class project. When you go back to school, please tell your fellow students how much I appreciate what you all did and the money you worked so hard to earn. It encourages me in my work when young people take an interest in Crazy Horse and what we're doing here. We get letters from young people all around the country. Even some from abroad. I read all of them, too. Yes, I appreciate your interest very much."

"Adam, this is very good beef," said Monique.

"Is this that cow that gave you so much trouble?" asked Korczak.

"Yes, sir. The one that stepped on my foot."

"It tastes pretty good for such a mean critter," said his father. "We once had 60 head of registered Holstein cattle here, Tom. Mother and I took care of them in the early days. It was a full-fledged dairy farm. That dairy supported this project in the early years. There weren't many visitors then, and I don't know how we'd have lived and continued the work on the mountain without the money from selling that milk.

"I built a beautiful milking parlor down there. First modern milking parlor in this area, they tell me. All sanitary containers for storing the milk. Right up town! We were very proud of it, but it was hard work. The children will tell you. When they were old enough, they helped with the milking and tending the cattle."

Tom noticed all the young people were very quiet at the table, not interrupting their father when he was talking. They seemed to have a sort of facial sign language that worked among them. Tom also noticed everyone was eating diced raw onions. A big bowl of them had been passed, and now it was going around again. Tom didn't like onions, especially raw onions. Korczak noticed he hadn't taken any. "We eat onions here like fresh fruit. They're very healthy for you, you know."

45

Tom didn't want to have to eat raw onions, so he tried to change the subject. "Where did all your children go to school?"

"At the Crazy Horse School!" came a chorus of young voices from around the table.

"They'll tell you about it," said Korczak. "We had our own school right here. It's just on the other side of the parking lot. You can see it down there. Have you ever seen an old-fashioned one-room country school? That's what we had. It was the old Evergreen School several miles from here. It was built in the late 1800's. It was no longer in use, so I bought it, and we moved it here. Six of the youngsters went to school there. We had a certified teacher."

"Mrs. Griffith," said Adam. "She was very nice."

"She was pretty strict," said Cas. "You couldn't get away with anything."

"I seem to recall you got away with quite a bit," laughed Anne. "Remember how we'd keep playing in the woods pretending we didn't hear the school bell ringing?"

The daily flag-raising at the Crazy Horse School

46

Cas said, "I remember having to haul in wood for the stove in the winter."

Joel said, "I remember those cold outhouses in the winter." Everyone laughed.

Adam said, "I liked the piano. Mrs. Griffith would play, and teach us all kinds of songs."

Jadwiga added, "We always did special songs for Christmas. Remember those Christmas plays we did? Those were fun."

"And every day we'd have a little ceremony putting up the flag," said Anne.

"You'll always see the American flag flying at Crazy Horse," said Korczak. "We do a lot of things wrong, but this still is the greatest country in the world.

"It was very practical to have that school. With all the youngsters in school at one time, it just made good sense to have our own school. We were like Mother Hubbard, but we knew what to do.

"Before we got the schoolhouse, the children went to school in town. We were so poor then, when Mother would pick them up, they'd stop and pick up empty pop bottles from the ditches along the road on the way home. We'd sell them. Oh, it was very humble here in the beginning, Tom. Very humble indeed."

As the young people finished their lunch, they quietly carried their plates and dishes to the kitchen. Ruth had not eaten, but had been coming and going.

"Mother, won't you sit down and join us?" asked Korczak. She wrinkled her nose at him. He turned to Tom. "Mother just works all the time. I can never get her to rest. She has all these children to help her, but she'd rather do things herself. Isn't that right, Mother?"

"No, it isn't, but I'm not going to argue with you!" She smiled, and patted him on the shoulder. She didn't sit down, either. "Would you like a cup of coffee and maybe a piece of hot apple pie?"

"That sounds good. Yes, please, Mother. How about you, Tom? You'll have some pie with me, won't you. The youngsters have to eat theirs and get back to work, but you and I can sit here and talk a little."

Adam, Cas and Joel stood by the door, and Korczak said, "Back to the salt mine, fellows?"

"Yes, sir," said Adam.

"Now, those holes you drilled this morning are 10 feet deep. Right?" Korczak's voice was all business now.

"Yes, sir, and just at the angle you told us," said Cas. He took a pencil and paper and quickly sketched a network of little circles and lines showing the number of holes and their angle to the mountain. "They're just like this."

Korczak studied the sketch, and said, "Good. That's just right to take the rock out the way we want it. All right, you fellows finish up with that. How many holes do you have yet to drill?"

"We did 15 this morning, and we have five left to drill."

"All right. You finish up, and then we'll load. We should be able to have that blast this afternoon," Korczak said.

"Yes, sir. I don't see any problem," said Cas.

"That is the problem!" retorted his father, only half joking. "All of you have to learn to see the problems before they become problems. I wish you'd remember that. Now, you three be careful up there. Keep those hard hats on, and I want to see you wearing ear plugs to protect your ears from those loud jackhammers. And, be VERY careful!"

The trio nodded, and filed out to return to the mountain. "That's very dangerous work up there. Very dangerous. I don't worry about myself, but I worry about them up there. But, they grew up on that mountain, and I guess they're pretty fearless. You have to respect that mountain. You never can take it for granted . . . ."

Korczak gazed out the big window at the distant mountain. It had changed color to a light tan in the midday sky in which a few clouds were forming. Ruth had brought the pie and coffee, and then disappeared. The room was quiet with the others gone. There was only the murmur of the visitors in the other part of the complex.

"I like it when it's like this," said Korczak. "Now we can talk a little. I'll bet you have some questions."

Tom nodded. "Yes, sir. The last day of school my classmates all made a list for me of things they wanted to know. They thought I might forget what to ask. I brought it, but I forgot it in the car."

Korczak laughed. His eyes sparkled and the big beard swept across his chest when he turned his head from side to side. "That's usually the way with lists. Mother always is making them. So do most of the reporters who come here. They might not like to admit it, but they also make a little list of questions so they won't forget. I'll bet you remember your questions. I don't know if I can answer them, but I'll try. Go ahead. Shoot."

CHAPTER 6

STANDING BEAR'S INVITATION

W hy am I carving Crazy Horse? That's a very good question. The answer is a rather unusual story." Korczak stroked his beard slowly and looked at Tom with narrowed eyes.

"The story began in 1939—way before you were born. That was the year that marble portrait of Paderewski won first prize by popular vote at the New York World's Fair. Nobody was more surprised than I was."

"The head you carved in five days?" asked Tom.

"Five and one-half days. In my basement under a 60-watt light bulb. It was done in a fury. I didn't even make a clay study for it. I never met Paderewski, so that portrait was made from photographs. I had a chance to meet him once. He asked for me to come visit him, but I said, 'no.' I was very young then. What did I have to say to such a great man as that? Later, I always wished I had gone. He was so remarkable.

"That same year, 1939, I made my first trip to the Black Hills. In early summer I worked briefly as assistant sculptor to Gutzon Borglum at Mt. Rushmore. Oh, Mr. Borglum was a great man. I could talk about him all day. We were both members of the National Sculpture Society. But, that's another story. I will say one thing: if it hadn't been for Gutzon Borglum's work at Mt. Rushmore, I never could have moved one piece of rock to build a memorial to the Indians in the Black Hills.

"It was ironic that I should come out here to work with him. You see, when I

49

was 13 years old, I had read about Mr. Borglum's plans to carve a mountain in Georgia. I thought carving a mountain was something I would like very much to do when I grew up. I wanted to be a sculptor. Wasn't it unusual that 18 years later I would have the chance to work with Mr. Borglum on a mountain carving?

"I didn't get to work on it for long. Only about two and one-half months. It seems I got into a pretty bad fight with Mr. Borglum's son, and Mr. Borglum had to fire me. I'm very proud of Mr. Borglum's letter where he 'fired' me. He said some very fine things. In fact, I've had an enlarged copy made of it, and it hangs in my room for everyone to see. Well, I packed up the few things I'd brought out, and went back East to my home in West Hartford, Connecticut.

Tom listens intently as Korczak answers the boy's questions

"A short time later, out of the blue, I got a curious letter from a person named Chief Henry Standing Bear. He lived on the Pine Ridge Reservation here in South Dakota. He said he understood I'd won the first prize at the World's Fair with Paderewski, and I guess he knew I'd worked at Mt. Rushmore. Standing Bear said the Indians wanted a mountain carving to honor one of their great chiefs, Crazy Horse. He asked if I'd be interested in carving such a memorial for them.

"Well, Tom, I'd never heard of this Standing Bear. To carve a mountain is no small thing, so I just thought someone must be playing a practical joke. I'm not sure I even answered that first letter. But, pretty soon Standing Bear wrote another letter, again asking me to carve a mountain. In that second letter he wrote, 'My Fellow Chiefs and I would like the White Man to know the Red Man had great heroes, too.'

"Tom, you must admit, that's an interesting sentence. Very interesting. Mind you, at the time I knew nothing whatsoever about Indians. In fact, I thought they were all gone—like the dodo bird. His second letter made me curious, though—especially that one line. I answered Standing Bear that I was thinking about it, and asked him for more details. In the meantime, I went to the library to see what I could find out about Indians. I always loved to go to a library.

"I looked up Crazy Horse in the encyclopedia. There wasn't much information, but what I found was very interesting. It said he was an unusual leader, and

50

that he was one of the Sioux chiefs who defeated Custer at the Battle of Little Big Horn. Of course, I'd heard of that famous battle, but it was news to me Crazy Horse had anything to do with it. I thought it was all Sitting Bull.

"In the encyclopedia it told how the Indians called Crazy Horse their 'strange one,' and how they respected and followed him. It also said as a boy his name was Curly because his hair was long and wavy. It was much lighter in color than other Indians. It was his father who was called Crazy Horse, but he was so proud of Curly, the father took the name, Worm. He gave his own name, Crazy Horse, to his son.

"Don't you think that's rather an unusual thing, Tom?" asked Korczak, his voice very emotional. "To give away his own name!"

Tom replied, "Curly must have done something very special for his father to do that, to take a name like Worm."

"Exactly," said Korczak. "I was intrigued. So, I took some books about Indians home with me. Was I in for a surprise. Tom, you've heard of the Boy Scouts and the Girl Scouts?"

"Oh, sure," said the boy. "I'm a Scout. Troop 15."

"There you are! Do you know what you learn in the Scouts? Indian lore! The old Indian tradition is what scouting is all about. Living in the wilderness, tracking, cooking, observing Nature. I had been a Scoutmaster in Boston, and almost everything we studied in scouting came from the Indians."

"I guess that's right," said Tom. "We learned to make a bow and arrow when I was a Cub Scout. And, how to fish with a spear. We tried to make some things like I saw in your Indian Museum."

"Well, those books told how the Indians made and used all those things centuries before we white men came to this country. I also learned the Indians made great contributions to our way of life. Do you know where we got corn, potatoes, squash, turnips and tobacco? From the Indians. They had all those things before we came here, and they gave them to the white man. Willingly. When the Pilgrims landed here, it was the Indians who saved them from starving. Brought them all kinds of food the white man never knew before. Even wild turkeys, which is why we still eat turkey on Thanksgiving. Ben Franklin wanted the turkey to be our national bird.

"Those books I was studying also told how the federal government had made treaties with the various Indian tribes, and then systematically broke each treaty. It was the first time I learned about that famous Treaty of 1868. In that treaty the President of the United States said, 'As long as rivers run and grass grows and trees bear leaves, Paha Sapa—the Black Hills of Dakota—will forever be the sacred land of the Sioux Indians.'

"But, Tom, after gold was discovered in the Black Hills, just a few miles from where we're sitting now, the white men came and took the Black Hills. I was surprised to learn there was a real gold rush here in 1874 to 1876, and thousands of white men came to get rich. Settlements and towns sprang up everywhere, and the government did nothing to stop them. It broke its treaty with the Indians, who were sent to reservations. They were lands the white man didn't want.

"Of course the Indians tried to defend themselves in every way they could.

51

The Indian always had lived off the land, but with the taking of his land and the slaughter of the buffalo, it was the end of the trail for the Indian. It was just a matter of time.

"I read about all these things, and I didn't know what to think. Tom, I'm a storyteller in stone. That's all I am, and this story of the American Indian had begun to interest me more than a little. And, there seemed to be a bit of a mystery about this fellow, Crazy Horse. You remember, ever since I was 13, I had wanted to carve a mountain. I started to give the invitation from this Indian more serious thought.

"Standing Bear and I had been exchanging letters, and in the spring of 1940, I decided to come back to South Dakota to meet him to find out more about this Indian Memorial he kept asking me to carve from a mountain."

While Korczak was telling the story, Ruth had looked in several times. Now she asked if he'd like another cup of coffee. "Yes, dear. I'll take a little more. I'll bet Tom would like another soft drink. The pie was delicious, but you know it has lots of calories. Tom, why don't you move around here to Ruth's rocking chair. It's more comfortable, and Mother isn't going to join us. I wish she would."

As Tom moved around the long table, Korczak lit another cigar, and continued the story of why he decided to carve the mountain.

"Gasoline only cost about eight or nine cents a gallon then, and I decided to drive out. I arrived on the Pine Ridge Reservation in March, 1940. It was about the most desolate, lonely place I'd ever seen. There weren't any hotels or motels. Just one brick building where the government agent lived. The rest were a few wooden buildings, pretty dilapidated. There wasn't any snow and it wasn't too cold, but the wind blew all the time. It didn't look like anything would grow. The dirt and dust were terrible. I thought it looked like the end of the world. I asked myself, 'Is this where we put the Indians?' I couldn't believe it.

"Standing Bear and his lovely wife lived in a rather neat tiny white house set back a little off the main street. There wasn't any room for me, so I slept in the car. I was on the Pine Ridge for three weeks, and I slept in my car the whole time."

"Had you ever met an Indian before?" asked Tom.

"No. Really, I didn't know sickum from come here about Indians. All I knew was what little bit I'd read. I wasn't quite sure they still existed. That was one of the things I wanted to learn by coming to Pine Ridge. Also, I was very curious about this mysterious Crazy Horse. I kept thinking about what Standing Bear had written, 'My Fellow Chiefs and I would like the White Man to know the Red Man had great heroes, too.' What a story line that is."

"Was Standing Bear a real Indian?" asked the boy. He was listening intently to Korczak's story, his elbows on the table and his chin resting on his hands.

"Oh, yes. Indeed. He was a full blooded Sioux Indian. His skin was a rich full-blooded mahogany color, very shiny. An interesting color."

"Did he speak in Sioux?" Tom asked.

"Yes. He spoke Lakota. That's the proper word. Sioux is a French word. Henry spoke Lakota, but also spoke English very well. He gestured a lot and spoke very slowly. He would apologize for his English, but he didn't need to.

"I've always been a sucker for a left!" says
Korczak

Henry was a well educated man. He graduated from Carlisle University. His brother, Luther Standing Bear, had graduated from the first class at Carlisle. Luther had become quite famous in Hollywood. He wrote books about Indian life that were translated into several languages. He illustrated many of them himself. In one of his books he mentions the idea for an Indian memorial similar to what we're doing here.

"When Henry spoke about Crazy Horse, it was with great reverence. Henry was a direct descendent of Crazy Horse, a distant cousin. Although Crazy Horse had no children who lived to maturity, Henry was descended from one of Crazy Horse's uncles. When Henry told me this, he also told me of an Indian tradition that had a great influence on my decision to carve that mountain.

"Standing Bear explained that the Indian has a concept of honoring their great that's totally different from the white man's. It was difficult for me to understand at first. It seems with the Indians only a relative of a great man has the right to honor that man or build a memorial to him. Other people who are not relatives have no right to honor that great man because somehow those people might have evil motives, want to get something out of it.

"It is a rather beautiful way. We white people do it the opposite. Relatives do not seek to build a memorial to a great man. We get a group of citizens together, and have them do it. We go through the back door. The Indian uses the direct approach. He says: that man was my ancestor, and he was a great man, so we should honor him—I would not lie or cheat because I am his blood.

"You know, Tom, I bought that. Isn't that the right way? No politics."

"So Standing Bear could ask to honor Crazy Horse because he was related to him?" said Tom with a serious expression.

"That's it. Oh, that had a lot of impact on me. I've always been a sucker for a left, but something about that concept of honoring your own really hit home to me."

A melodic chime broke in on them as the big, gold-faced clock behind

53

Korczak rang out the hour. Korczak paused, puffing his cigar. The smoke drifted up in wisps.

"Did Standing Bear know Crazy Horse?" Tom asked.

"No, but Standing Bear's father had known Crazy Horse. Thus Henry knew a great deal about his great ancestor, Tashunka Witco. That's Crazy Horse's name in Lakota. I remember him telling me how the Indians called Crazy Horse their 'silent one' or 'strange one' because Crazy Horse was a very quiet man. He never said much. He didn't participate in camp activities or the councils. He always wanted to stay apart by himself.

"As Standing Bear described him, he wasn't a very tall man. Only about 5'7" or 5'8", rather slight. He only weighed about 160 pounds. Sioux Indians were usually much larger in stature. As I told you, he was lighter than most Indians, and was called Curly because of his wavy hair. Well, it seemed this boy, Curly, would distinguish himself in everything he would do. Hunting, fishing and all the things Indian boys did.

"Standing Bear confirmed the story I'd read in the encyclopedia about Crazy Horse's father giving the son his own name. He told the story with great conviction.

"When he was older, Crazy Horse always could go out and bring back food for his tribe in the winter when no one else could find food. He could always get a deer or a buffalo. He always would go out alone, but often others would follow. This was how he became a chief, although he was very young.

"As Standing Bear explained it, a chief was not elected as we pick our leaders. A man became a chief if he was the most skilled at whatever he did. If you were the best hunter or the best warrior or the best medicine man, others would follow you. As long as you could produce for the tribe, you would be a chief. You see, the Plains Indians were nomads. They didn't live in one place, but they roamed the plains following the food and water supplies and the seasons. They lived from day to day, and those who could provide for them were their leaders.

"Crazy Horse was so skilled at so many things, he became a chief even though he didn't want to be one. He was just a natural leader, and the other Indians wanted to follow him. Since he was such a young man, I don't suppose some of the older Indians much liked the idea of following someone his age, but he was the most skilled, so his people wanted to follow him.

"He was not a council chief, but a war chief. Crazy Horse was a natural military leader. Standing Bear told how he would plan military strategy using decoys to lure his enemies into a trap where he could take them by surprise. Crazy Horse is the first Indian we know of to use the decoy system. It was very successful, although Standing Bear didn't talk much about the battles. He and the others would never mention the Battle of the Little Big Horn, I guess because they won the battle but lost the war.

"He talked with great admiration about Crazy Horse's bravery. He would be at the front of his warriors and enter battle crying, 'It's a good day to die.' It was a curious thing, but he never wore a warbonnet. Didn't own one. Only a single feather in his hair. He did become a hair shirt warrior, the Indians' highest honor, but it was taken away from him.

"Crazy Horse had another brilliant military idea. He never wanted warriors over about the age of 22 years. From about 15 years to 22 years was perfect. They would obey orders without question. Older men had their own ideas.

"Also, Crazy Horse never abandoned his wounded.

"Standing Bear talked so much about Crazy Horse's great military abilities I could hardly believe my ears, Tom. Remember this was a whole new world to me in 1940 on Pine Ridge. Years later I read that President Dwight Eisenhower, a five-star general, said Crazy Horse was the greatest cavalry leader since the Greeks. That's what they teach at the West Point Military Academy. Since the Greeks! That's something for Eisenhower to say.

"During those weeks I was in Pine Ridge, Standing Bear told me this story in bits and pieces. As I mentioned, he spoke very slowly and deliberately. There would be long pauses when he seemed to be in a trance. I would wait and wait. Finally, he would continue. We would talk day after day, and besides telling about Crazy Horse he talked about the traditional Indian way of life.

"He spoke very reverently about the Great Spirit, although I didn't understand much about that concept at the time. He did say all Indians everywhere in this nation worshiped the Great Spirit, and he said there never had been a religious war among the Indian tribes.

"To the Indian, the Earth was the Mother, and the sun, moon and stars—all relatives. Everything was a circle. A circle of life. He told how the Indians took care of Nature, taking from it only what was needed for their existence. One thing I remember so well was his telling about the buffalo. Without the buffalo the Plains Indians could not live. Of course, when the white man came, he slaughtered all the buffalo. Buffalo Bill alone killed about 2,800 in one eight-month period.

"The Indian killed only what buffalo he needed. Standing Bear told how when the Indian took a buffalo, he would turn its head to the east and thank the buffalo for its meat. Every part of the animal was used. Nothing was wasted. The meat was for food, the bones for utensils, jewelry and weapons, the hide was for shelter and clothing. Some parts were for medicine.

"Standing Bear also talked about the craftsmanship of the Indians. How they made the beautiful things you saw in that museum out there. Wonderfully beaded and quilled clothing and moccasins, intricately woven baskets and blankets. Tools and practical items for the household. So many things. All by hand. All from Nature.

"Henry spoke passionately about the Paha Sapa, the Black Hills. They were sacred to the Sioux Indians. To them the Hills were like a cathedral, a sanctuary, their sacred ground. They never lived in the Hills, but would come here only to worship, to hunt and gather berries and edible plants or to get tipi poles.

"Standing Bear grew very angry when he spoke of the broken treaty of 1868. That was the one I'd read about in which the President promised the Black Hills would belong to the Indians forever. I remember how his old eyes flashed out of that dark mahogany face, then he would shake his head and fall silent for a long while.

"After a couple of weeks, I understood why Crazy Horse was a heroic figure to Standing Bear and the others. He had fought valiantly to defend his people and their way of life in the only manner he knew. He never surrendered, never signed a treaty, he had never gone on the reservation. I realized, also, Crazy Horse was a symbol of everything the Indian had stood for and lost, his whole way of life. Most of it was already gone in 1939. Oh, Tom you wouldn't believe how desolate that reservation was. Poverty-stricken in every way. It hasn't changed much in all these years since.

"Of all the stories Standing Bear told me, one seemed to sum up the whole character of this remarkable man called Crazy Horse: the year after the Battle of Little Big Horn and after all his followers had gone on the reservation, Crazy Horse remained free. The soldiers were searching for him everywhere, but they couldn't catch him.

"One day on the prairie Crazy Horse met a white trader who spoke Lakota. This trader mocked Crazy Horse and made fun of him, saying, 'Where are your lands now, Crazy Horse? All your people are captured and put on reservations. Where are your lands you fought for?' " Korczak's voice grew much softer and very emotional. Tom drew closer.

"It was a beautiful September morning. The sun wasn't too high in a clear sky. It was still and rather warm, just a touch of autumn in the air. Crazy Horse, sitting on his pony, said nothing for awhile. He just stared at this white trader. Then, he slowly raised his arm and pointed out over his horse's head to the east, and said proudly, 'My lands are where my dead lie buried.' "

Korczak's voice broke. A small tear slid down his furrowed cheek and trickled into his beard. He continued very softly, "I can hardly tell that story. I get all choked up. Every time. What a story that is!"

"That's why he's pointing over the horse's head?" said Tom quietly.

"That's why he's pointing. To his lands. Of course, they were all taken when he said that, but as far as you could see in every direction those had been the lands of the Indians. 'My lands are where my dead lie buried,' that's the tragic story of the American Indian in one sentence. It marked the end of Crazy Horse and the end of a beautiful way of life for a proud race of people that had lived here for untold centuries.

"That same day Crazy Horse went to Fort Robinson in Nebraska under a flag of truce to talk about provisions for his people. He was stabbed in the back by a white soldier, and he died early the next morning, September 6, 1877. Crazy Horse was only 33 or 34 years old."

CHAPTER 7

STORYTELLER IN STONE

After three weeks I got in my car and drove back to my home in West Hartford, Connecticut. My visit in Pine Ridge had a tremendous impact on me. I don't know that I went away with any great understanding of the Indian or with much knowledge of him, but I went away knowing he was a race of people apart from us whose story certainly should be told.

"Although I'd dreamed of carving a mountain, I wanted to think it over. You know carving a mountain is not something you undertake lightly. Even then I knew that. And, there were many problems.

"Standing Bear insisted the Indian Memorial be in the Paha Sapa, the Black Hills. I told him I didn't like the rock, and thought it should be as far away from Mt. Rushmore as possible, perhaps in the Grand Tetons of Wyoming where the rock was so much harder. I also knew Indians were not very popular in South Dakota, so an Indian Memorial wouldn't be greeted with open arms. I had many good reasons, but they made no difference to him. It had to be in the Black Hills.

"I also thought it should be more than a mountain carving. Somehow it should be a humanitarian project to benefit the Indian people. That didn't interest him either. All Standing Bear wanted was his great ancestor carved on a mountain in the Black Hills.

"There also were the very big questions of how to get a mountain and how to pay for the carving. I knew first hand the very great difficulties Mr. Borglum had to overcome with the federal government in trying to carve Mt. Rushmore, and I didn't want any part of the government involved in Crazy Horse. I found out later Henry assumed the Indian Memorial would be a federal project and that I would have all the help I needed from the Indian people.

"So, I went home that spring of 1940 with nothing decided. When I got back, I had a big project waiting for me. That was the *Noah Webster* statue. Did Mother tell you about that?"

"Yes, sir," replied Tom. "And, we looked at all the pictures of you working on the big scaffolds. That's a huge statue."

"Thirteen and one-half feet. That turned out to be quite a job. I never dreamed it would take two years of my life! Then I gave it away. That's a long story we'll save for another day. It makes me weary just to think of it.

"While I was making it, I didn't forget about the Indians' invitation. I was studying everything I could find about Indians. I even made a clay study for Crazy Horse, based on that story Standing Bear told of 'My lands are where my dead lie buried.' Standing Bear came East to look at it. He stayed at my home, and we talked more about the mountain carving he wanted me to do.

"I also showed him the mahogany portrait I had carved of him. He loved that portrait. Twenty-three years later I gave it as a gift to President John F. Kennedy when he visited South Dakota. It's in the J. F. Kennedy Memorial Library in Boston today. There's a wonderful moment about that head I'll never forget.

"After I'd presented the portrait to President Kennedy, the Secretary of the Interior said he'd have the head packed and shipped back to Washington. The President turned to him, and said, 'You'll do no such thing! I'm taking this beautiful work home with me.' And he did. They carried it over, and put it in the back seat of the President's big black limousine.

"The last time I saw that head of Standing Bear it was on the back seat with the President of the United States. I said to myself, 'Henry, if you could see yourself now! Riding in that big limousine with the President of the United States. You've come a long way, Henry . . . .' " Korczak threw back his head and roared with laughter. "I think he'd have been very proud.

"I continued to work on the Noah Webster statue, but all the while I was reading everything I could get my hands on about Indians. I was always thinking about the invitation to come to the Black Hills to carve Crazy Horse.

"Then, the dogs of war were unleashed, and America entered the Second World War. I was 36 years old, but I volunteered in the Army—and they took me. I landed on Omaha Beach. Maybe you've heard of that. It was very bad. None of us thought we'd make it. I pray your generation never has to fight a war, Tom.

"Later, I was blown up a couple of times, and spent several weeks in a hospital. My mind always would come back to Crazy Horse. In the midst of this world conflict, I kept thinking about what an idyllic life the American Indian had led. He, too, was thrust into a great war. A war with the white man that the Indian could not win. Crazy Horse knew it was the end of the trail. That's why he would never surrender and refused to go on the reservation. He stood for the traditional way of life for his people that he knew was vanishing before his eyes."

Korczak's voice had grown very emotional again. There was a long pause before he went on. "When the war finally ended in 1945, the government offered me a wonderful sculptural commission to make war memorials in Europe—all the way from Omaha Beach and Utah Beach to Berlin. Oh, it was a very, very tempting offer. What every sculptor dreams of.

"All the marble and help I wanted. But, I turned it down. It wasn't too difficult, really. You see, Tom, I'd decided to accept the Indians' invitation to carve a

KORCZAK ©

CHIEF HENRY STANDING BEAR
Heroic Size African Mahogany   1940
John F. Kennedy Memorial Library
Boston, Massachusettes

mountain to their great chief, a symbol of the American Indian.

"I'd wanted to carve a mountain since I was 13. Now there was a reason to do it. A very good reason. For a vanishing race of people, for a way of life that had disappeared from the face of the earth. Me being the romantic soul that I am, I could not think of anything greater than that. I'm a crusader for lost causes, and I really fell for this Crazy Horse.

"All my friends were building memorials in Washington, D.C., in Williamsburg, Virginia, or other places, but I didn't care about those memorials or even all the war memorials in Europe. To carve a mountain—that was different. To tell the story of the American Indian. That's what I wanted to do. Remember, I'd read everything I could get and I'd been thinking about this for six years already. I didn't know how I was going to do it, but I knew I was going to try. And, I also knew it was going to be a humanitarian undertaking, something more than just a mountain sculpture.

"What else did I have to do with my life?" Korczak's big fist slammed down on the table upsetting his coffee cup, which clattered in its saucer. Tom jumped. Korczak leaned toward him. "What else? When I'd been asked by these old Indians to come out here and tell the story of their great chief. To tell the story on a mountain of a race of people that once lived. What an honor! For a little Polish-American orphan boy from Boston. What an honor!" Korczak's voice trailed off. His eyes were moist. "I'm sorry. I get too emotional. But, it's what you asked. Why am I carving Crazy Horse? I'm a storyteller in stone. That's what I'm doing up there on that mountain. I'm telling the story of a race of people that once lived. Not just Crazy Horse, but the story of the North American Indians. So the world will not forget. Long after you and I are gone, that mountain will still be there telling their story. That's why I'm carving Crazy Horse."

Korczak stopped, crushing out his cigar. The room fell silent. Clouds were building over the mountain.

"Mother says I get a little carried away sometimes, but you asked the most important question of all. Why am I doing it? Why have I devoted my life to this? I hope that long story answered your question. Did it help you understand?"

"Oh, yes, sir," replied Tom enthusiastically . He leaned back in the rocker. "I wish it were all written down so I could take it back to my class to read. The mountain carving is sort of like history, isn't it?"

"Yes, Tom. It's very much like history. If I were a writer, I'd write it all in a story. But, I'm a sculptor, so I'm carving it on a big mountain. Doesn't it amount to the same thing?"

"Everyone will be able to read it on the mountain," said Tom.

"Funny you should put it that way. I often say I write in stone so those who run can read. We live in such a busy world, lots of people don't take the time to read books. I wish they would, but they don't. So, when Crazy Horse rides out of that big mountain, people from all over the world no matter what language they speak, will be able to read about him in the stone. It will tell the story. And, the Museum will be here to tell all about the Indian culture. If we're going to live in the present for the future, we must have an understanding of the past. The world must not forget the American Indian."

CHAPTER 8

PIONEERING IN THE WILDERNESS

See that thunderhead building over the mountain?" said Korczak. "That's how the mountain got its name. After the war I came back out here in 1946. Standing Bear met me, and we started searching for a mountain to carve. I still wanted to do it somewhere else, anywhere away from Mt. Rushmore. I didn't want people making comparisons all the time or thinking there was some kind of competition. There never has been. But, Standing Bear wouldn't listen to me. It had to be in Paha Sapa.

"We searched and searched. We climbed more mountains than I could count. Then, one day we found this mountain. It had a big thunderhead just like that one out there. I named it Thunderhead Mountain. It never had a name before that. Those big clouds often come about this time of the day, but they'll break up. It won't rain."

"It's not Crazy Horse Mountain?" asked Tom.

"No, but everyone calls it that. It's all right, but the real name is Thunderhead Mountain."

"Did you buy the mountain?" asked the boy.

"Not the way you're thinking, no. It belonged to the federal government, and I got it on a mining claim. That meant I had it as long as I did a certain amount of mining up there every year. I had claimed it, which was very common practice."

"Like staking out a claim for gold? I've heard of that," Tom said.

"Yes. Mining for any kind of mineral. There are plenty of them up there. To the government moving rock is mining. The government couldn't care less if the mountain looks like an Indian when I'm done moving rock. Just as long as I mine every year. They call it assessment work. I think that's pretty funny.

"Years later, the non-profit Crazy Horse Memorial Foundation bought 328 acres around the mountain from the U.S. government by means of a land exchange. You know, it's kind of funny. I had to buy that land from the state to trade with the federal government to give it back to the Indians we stole it all from in the first place.

"After I'd picked out the mountain, I bought about 640 acres down here. It took practically every penny I had. That's why I only had $174 left to start the project. There's a funny story about how I bought this land down here. It's funny now. It wasn't funny at the time.

"It seems they had a system of measurement out here called 'metes and bounds.' I'd never heard of that, but it's how they measured property. They'd put a rock or something where one piece of property met the other, and that was where the boundary was. Metes and bounds. Well, when I bought this land it was 360 acres 'more or less.' Some arrangement! After I paid for it, we actually measured the property. What do you suppose we discovered? It was about 40 acres LESS. Imagine what those 40 acres would be worth today.

"Tom, what would you think if you bought a big bag of 360 marbles, and when you got home and counted, you found you only had 320? You wouldn't be very happy. I learned the hard way. So, watch out if someone tries to sell you something 'more or less.' In the Bible it says, 'A stranger came, so I took him in.'

The old army tent in which Korczak lived his first seven months at Crazy Horse

Out here they have a variation on that. It goes, 'A stranger came, so I took him!' "

Tom said, "You got took for 40 acres."

"I sure got took." Korczak laughed. "Some beginning, huh? I was a lot more careful after that. Oh, I could tell you lots of stories like that. Some people around here don't like Indians very much. They don't like it that I'm carving an Indian on that mountain. When I came out here, I had no conception of their hatred for the Indian. They've tried to make things very difficult for Mother and me. Oh, yes. But, I don't complain. It does hurt a little, though."

"If you didn't have any money left when you got here, how did you get started?" asked Tom.

"See these hands," Korczak said, holding them up. "They're pretty old and gnarled now, but they were strong then. My back was, too. That was before all the operations on it.

Korczak pioneering, notching logs in 1947 for his original studio-home

"That's the tent I lived in the first seven months. In that picture right over there. I arrived out here to stay on May 3, 1947. About all I had was that tent, a beat up old Army jeep, $174 and a dream. You'll have to admit that's a pretty humble beginning.

"There was nothing here. Just rocks and trees. Not even a road. So, I lived in that tent while I built that big room in there where the piano is."

"The log cabin," said Tom. "It's sure different from any log cabin I ever imagined. I thought it would be tiny."

"Some of those logs run 70 to 80 feet long. There's one running through the kitchen. See it? That goes clear across the big room. It was something to build that log cabin. I cut down the trees by hand, and Mother helped peel the bark off. We weren't married then. She and a few others came out with me from the East. She was the only one who stayed, even when I asked her to go home.

"After I notched the logs, I used the old jeep I bought to pull them up the walls. It took all summer to put up the cabin. Then we had to hurry and get all the caulking between the logs to keep out the cold and snow before winter. We worked like beavers here that first summer to get a place ready to live in that winter. It was real pioneering. This was a wilderness.

"Do you know what the hardest part was? Getting used to the altitude. Where I lived in West Hartford, Connecticut, was almost sea level. Here, it's 6,240 feet above sea level where we're sitting. That's well over a mile high. The top of the mountain is 6,740 feet! The air is very thin. I'd cut down one tree, and I'd have to stop and rest. Then, I'd cut another, then rest again. It took a long time to get used to this altitude. I've been up here so long now it's hard for me to go back to sea level again."

Tom rocked slowly back and forth in his chair, and said, "I think your log cabin is very beautiful."

"It almost didn't get built. I got here on May 3rd, and the first week in June it snowed. Would you believe it? When I came out of that tent one morning, everything was white. The ground, the rocks, the trees, even the mountain was all white. It even was stacked in little piles on top of the fenceposts. A heavy, wet snow about three inches deep.

"I thought 'What kind of place is this? What have I gotten myself into? You can't carve a mountain in a place where it snows in June!' But, I couldn't let the old Indians down. I came out here to carve a mountain for them—snow or not. I had to try. We've had snow a few times in June, but it usually melts right away. A snow like that brings lots of needed moisture."

Tom was looking out the window at the big thunderhead over the mountain. He said, "You sure built lots of doors and windows in your house. I like all the natural light."

"Yes, there are plenty of windows and skylights. Most of the skylights face north to let in the even light all year. After my parents were killed when I was one year old, I lived in a dark, gloomy orphanage. The nuns were very strict. Later, I lived in foster homes. All during grade school I lived in a foster home in Cambridge, Massachusetts, a suburb of Boston. My foster father was an Irish prize fighter, who worked and played very hard. He had me mixing cement and pouring concrete when I was eight or nine years old. If I did something he didn't like, he'd just slug me." Korczak rubbed his chin. "The next thing I knew, he'd throw a bucket of water on me. I'd wake up 15 or 20 feet away where I'd landed. I'd shake my head a little, get up, and stagger back to work. He wasn't so bad, though, compared with his wife. She was not a nice person. She was the most frightening human being I've ever seen. She terrified me."

"Didn't you want to run away?" asked Tom.

"Every day I was there. But, Tom, nothing could be worse than that Home for Destitute Children. Nothing. I didn't want to go back there, so I stayed in the foster home.

"After I started school, I always liked to read. I loved books, and couldn't get enough of them. My room was in the attic of their house, and I always would go up there and read. Well, this mean woman didn't like me reading, and whenever she'd catch me with a book, she would beat me.

"At night I'd excuse myself and go to the attic. I never had a bed. I slept on wooden boxes. I'd crawl under my blanket and read by the light of a candle. I sold junk, iron, rags, you name it, and used the money to buy candles to read. I also had to buy all my own clothes with my junk money. They never bought me

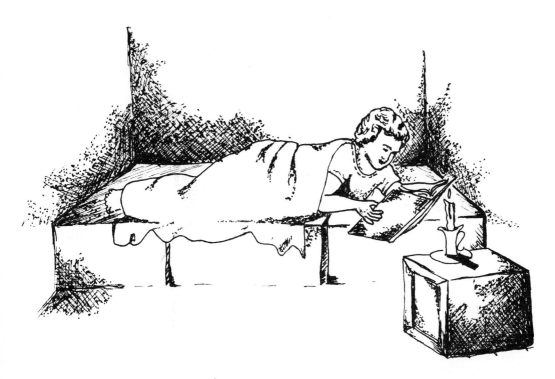

Reading by candlelight in the attic where Korczak slept on wooden boxes, listening for his cruel foster mother

anything. I had those boxes to sleep on, old crates, but no mattress, no sheets, nothing. I used old overcoats for a mattress and covers. I finally sold enough junk to buy myself a blanket. It got pretty cold up there in the winter. Well, anyway, I'd be under my blanket reading by the light of my candle. If I'd hear her coming up, I'd have to put out the candle quickly and pretend I was sleeping. That wax was hot! But, she never caught me. I said to myself if I ever built a house of my own when I grew up, there would be lots and lots of windows to let in the light. That's why you see so many skylights and windows in this house—even in that log cabin. That skylight runs the whole length of the north side of it. I've had enough darkness.

"Tom, she was a very cruel person. When this cruel woman really got mad, she'd throw knives at me. Long butcher knives. I was little, and was very quick. When she'd miss me, I'd just smile at her and say, 'You missed. Try again!' Then, I'd run as fast as I could. If she ever caught me, she'd tear off all my cothes and jump up and down on my back. She wore high heeled shoes, and they were very painful on my back. I still have scars today from her jumping up and down on me.

"I read my books in spite of her. It's a terrible thing not to let young people read. Books can be such great friends. All through life I've loved books. I read several at one time. I even carried two books with me in my knapsack all during the war: a book of Greek plays and the collected works of Shakespeare. I love biography and history books. I'll bet you like to read, Tom."

"Yes, I do. Very much," said the boy. "I want to read more about Crazy Horse."

"The best book about him is by Mari Sandoz. It's called *CRAZY HORSE, the Strange Man of the Oglalas*. She understood much of the Lakota language and visited with many people who knew Crazy Horse. I'll get Mother to give you a copy of that. You'll enjoy reading about him.

"I read by candlelight and kerosene lamps that first winter out here. There was no electricity, and we couldn't afford to have it brought in right away. It was so humble. We got our heat from that big fireplace in there, and we cooked on a wood-burning stove.

"Of course, there was no water. I couldn't afford to have a well dug, so I put a dirt dam down in the valley. Natural springs make a little creek there. It bubbles and murmurs along all year around. The Indians named it Laughing Water, because it reminded them of soft laughter as it bubbled along. When that dam got full, I carried water up here in 10-gallon cream cans. All that first winter. We didn't get a well until the next year. Now we have 14 wells to furnish water for all these visitors.

"There wasn't much money for food. We wanted to have a garden, but did you every try to grow anything at an altitude of 6,240 feet? This is about the highest private residence in the Black Hills, and gardening doesn't work very well. No way. There's little water and very short growing seasons. What little we did manage to grow was eaten by the deer and the rabbits. I had beautiful fruit trees in the East, but they wouldn't grow here.

"It's a funny thing, Tom. The white man could starve in this country, but the Indian would feast like a king. He ate the wonderful berries and those delicious roots. There are wild turnips here. I can't find them, but the Indians can. They are out of this world. The Indian would have no trouble eating here at all.

"We sure did, though. Since we couldn't raise a garden, we got some livestock: white leghorn chickens, a few cows and pigs and some horses for work and transportation. We got by. That was about all."

Tom said, "My grandparents have a farm with horses. I ride sometimes."

"You'd have loved my beautiful stallion, Warrior. A big golden palomino. He was more like a person than an animal. He understood whatever I'd say to him. Sometimes he'd pretend he didn't, just to tease me. I rode him up the other side of the mountain in the early years. There weren't any roads up there then. He'd wait up there for me all day, then race home with me in the evening.

"Warrior saved my life once. We were caught in a bad snowstorm. The snow was so deep he could hardly move, but he just kept going. Never stopped. If he'd stopped, we both would have died out there in the blizzard. I loved that horse.

"When he'd race down from the mountain after dusk, the sparks would fly off his hooves when they hit rocks. It was as if they were electric. He'd go like the wind, that golden mane and tail flying. Sometimes one of the children would ride with me, and the child would shout, 'Go faster, Daddy, go faster.' "

Tom thought pioneering sounded like a full time job, so he asked, "With all that to do here, did you have much time to work on the mountain?"

"I didn't. That was the sad part. I came out here to carve a mountain, not

Warrior racing down the mountain for home after a long day's work

build buildings and roads, but that was about all I got done those first two years. We had to have a place to live, didn't we? Then, we had to have a road in from the highway and a place for the visitors we hoped would come.

"No. I wasn't happy about it, but there was no time for the mountain the first year. The next year we had the first blast on the mountain. It only took off 10 tons, and that was the only blast that summer. It was for the official dedication of Crazy Horse on June 3rd, 1948. I'll never forget it. Five survivors of the Battle of Little Big Horn were here, and they told me all about Crazy Horse. They had known him and fought with him. I learned much from them.

"I wanted so badly to be up on the mountain working those first two years, but this down here had to be done. And, remember there was no way you could drive over to the mountain. I had to clear the timber to make a road over there. When I got to the mountain, there was no way to get up it.

"I didn't start regular work on the mountain until that third summer. And, was I ready! That's a very special mountain, Tom. I'm very happy when I'm up there working. I could stay up there all the time, but Mother likes to see me from time to time." Korczak stopped, and slammed both of his hands down on the arms of his chair. "Let's go up! Would you like to see it? Come on."

Tom's eyes grew wide in surprise and excitement. "Do you mean it? Really? Up the mountain with you?"

"Sure. I'll show you what I'm doing up there. Besides, I've been talking all the time, and I'll bet you have lots of questions I haven't given you a chance to ask. Mother says I talk too much."

"I really enjoy your stories. Everything here seems to have a story," said the boy.

"I guess you're right about that. Your class worked very hard, I know, to raise money to help me, and I want to show you why it costs so much up there. You'll be able to tell them how I used their money when you get back to school. Mother, where are you?"

Ruth wasn't far off, and when she ducked back into the room Korczak said, "Tom and I are going up the mountain." He stood up to get his jacket and the beat-up hat with the holes in it.

She said, "I think you'll have a very interesting time, Tom. I'll walk out with you two."

Tom got up from the comfortable rocker, and Korczak put his big arm around the boy's shoulders as they went out the door.

CHAPTER 9

SCULPTURE IN THE ROUND

That's the original model for Crazy Horse," said Korczak as they stepped outside, where it was bright and warm. They were in a courtyard-like patio surrounding a small patch of neatly trimmed lawn that looked like deep green carpet.

"Mother keeps this little lawn for me. Isn't it lovely? It's my touch of New England. We had such beautiful lawns back in Connecticut. They don't grow like that in this dry country."

To one side on a white wooden pedestal stood the Crazy Horse model. It was about 30 inches high, and was a warm pale grey with a pinkish tint. "That's Tennessee marble. Beautiful stone," said Korczak. "The sun brings out that unusual color. I cut that piece of stone from the *Noah Webster* statue in West Hartford."

"Did you make this before you made the big white model of Crazy Horse I saw this morning by the museum?" asked Tom.

"Oh, my, yes. I made this little one 20 years before the big plaster one out front. This marble model I made right after I got back from Europe after the war. This little one here was all we had out front to show the visitors what the mountain carving would look like. They had to use lots of imagination in those days. This little one was stolen from out there. It disappeared one night, and was gone about a year. Then, it came back. That's a curious story."

Ruth said, "If you start telling stories again, you'll never get up the mountain this afternoon."

CRAZY HORSE
Tennessee Marble   1946
1/300th scale model for
Crazy Horse mountain carving
Crazy Horse Memorial

"I told you how she is." Korczak winked at Tom, and slipped his arm around his energetic wife. They all walked across the little patio to a yellow open jeep. Tom thought it was going to be great fun to ride in it with Korczak. He jumped in eagerly.

As Korczak got behind the wheel, Ruth said, "You two have a good time. Remember, Tom's parents are coming back for him, so don't keep him up there listening to stories all night."

"Yes, Mother." He smiled, giving her a kiss on the forehead. The little jeep rumbled to life, and they set off.

Tom's first surprise was the long line-up of heavy equipment they passed. There were several big trucks, two bulldozers, a cement mixer, a couple more jeeps, a logging truck and many other big vehicles. All were bright yellow like the jeep, and each had its name painted on it in royal blue. Some of the names were: *Jupiter, Flapping Eagle, Old Mac, Big Rig, Faithful, Katz 'n Jammer, Archibald, Rosemary, The Lemon, Old Lady, Buster, Sheba, Alfie* and *Puff.*

Korczak stopped the jeep, gesturing toward all the vehicles. "This is just part of the heavy equipment we use here."

"To carve the mountain?" Tom inquired.

"Most of it. Yes. A lot of people still have the mistaken impression I'm up there with a hammer and chisel like some fancy sculptor in a comfortable studio in the East. I laugh. Some people will never understand mountain carving is a marriage of engineering and sculpture. I use all of this equipment, and I could use a lot more if I could afford it.

"This kind of equipment is very expensive, so we buy it used whenever I can get a good deal. You should have seen these vehicles when I got them. They were all beat up, some of them real junkers. We take them down to the garage, and during the winter we rebuild them, give them a nice coat of paint and, of course, name them. Everything has to have a name. Those are the Crazy Horse colors: blue and yellow. You might have seen them on the flag when you came in this morning."

"Do you rebuild them yourself?" asked Tom. He didn't think a sculptor fixed bulldozers and trucks.

"Sure," replied Korczak matter-of-factly. "How else would I get it done? You have to do many jobs in order to carve a mountain. I learned a little here and there over the years—when I worked in Boston on the waterfront as a young man and when I was in the Army."

Korczak eased the little jeep into gear. As they moved on, the mountain came into view again. The big thunderhead was breaking up, just as Korczak had predicted. They bounced on a dirt road down a little hill, and left the visitor complex behind.

As they passed a two-story frame building, Korczak said, "That's the old milking parlor. It was something in its day, but there isn't much time for cows now. Time is the most important thing we have, you know. Never forget that, Tom. Lost time cannot be made up."

They were entering the forest. The bumpy road wound through thick stands of tall ponderosa pine, swaying slightly in a little breeze that had come up. The air was fresh and clear, and Tom took a deep breath. It was like cold, fresh water on a hot, dry day.

They passed a little lake reflecting the stately trees and the blue sky and puffy clouds drifting above. Two ducks lifted off the lake, scolding the jeep with loud quacking. They shattered the reflections on the water.

"That's the second lake I built in the early years," said Korczak. "The first one is a much larger lake down that way. It's the one I carried the water from up to the house. Water is a very precious commodity in this country.

"It was down by that big lake the Indians gave me the name Brave Wolf. It

71

was quite a surprise to me. Man Afraid and some of his friends just came one day and asked to camp here. I took them down to the lake, and left them alone. I'd only been out here about four years, and I was very busy up on the mountain. I asked if they'd join me for supper, and that's when they gave me that name.

"In 1948 right after I came out here, the Indians at Pine Ridge wanted to give me an Indian name. I went down for a big pow-wow, but I asked them not to give me a name so soon. I said, 'It's a high honor for a white man to be given an Indian name. That honor should be earned, and I don't think I've done anything yet to deserve it. Please wait about 30 years, then, if you think I've done something worthwhile on the mountain, you can give me the name.' They weren't very happy with me, but they agreed to wait.

"It was two years later that this group came here, and did it as a surprise. It was an honor, and I was very pleased they wanted to do it. I promised them, as I had the others, I would do the job they invited me out here to do: carve their memorial for them."

"Did you like the name, Brave Wolf?" asked Tom.

"Oh, yes. Indeed. The wolf is a rather unusual animal in Nature's scheme of things. The Indians know that, and respect him. Speaking of animals, there's a deer."

Tom's eyes followed Korczak's pointing finger. At first he couldn't find it. Then he saw a slight movement. There were two deer, a mother and a fawn. The mother was light brown with a white tail. Her large ears stood tall and alert as her dark eyes studied them. The fawn was rust color with spots all over like white measles. They just stood and watched Korczak and Tom bounce past.

"They're not afraid. They know they're safe here. This is their home. We don't bother them. We have lots of wildlife here. You'll probably see more. Coyotes that howl in the night, wild turkeys, the biggest squirrels I've ever seen. They're very bold and mischievous rascals. We don't have any snakes, though. The altitude here is too high for them."

"I'm glad about that," said Tom, who didn't like snakes very much.

"That's Laughing Water running along the road. There's gold in that little stream. My children used to pan for it, and they'd usually find some. There are lots of red garnets, too.

"The first gold discovered in the Black Hills was only about five miles from here. It touched off gold fever. That was it for the Indians—treaties or no treaties. The second largest gold mine in the Western Hemisphere still operates in the Hills today—the Homestake at Lead.

"There's lots of gold on this property. A few years after I built that log cabin, I decided to put a little cellar under the kitchen. What do you suppose I hit? Yup! Gold. It assayed out very high gold content, too. But, I came out here to carve a mountain, not to go into the gold mining business."

Tom peered at Laughing Water, and asked, "Could I find gold in that stream?"

"Sure, but you'd have to work to find it. There's a story about two brothers who operated a market in a little town near here. One bought property on Laughing Water, and started raising chickens on it to butcher and sell in the

Panning for gold in Laughing Water

market in town. One day he took the chickens in, and while they were being cleaned, the brothers discovered gold nuggets the size of a fingernail in the chickens' craws. Pure gold nuggets!

"They closed the store immediately, and rushed off to search for gold. They never found where the chickens got it, but they always suspected it came from Laughing Water. If it's true—and I suspect it is—old Laughing Water got the last laugh."

They were getting closer to the mountain, which seemed to loom higher and higher as they approached it. They were crossing a little meadow of swaying tall grasses dotted with colorful flowers.

"Are all those wild flowers?" asked Tom.

"Yes. All wild. Beautiful, aren't they? Mother once walked back from the mountain, and picked 21 different kinds of flowers on the way home. I think this is just about the most beautiful country on earth. The Indians sure were lucky to have their sacred Paha Sapa." Korczak brought the jeep to a stop near another small body of water which reflected the mountain high above.

"Isn't that a beaver dam?" asked Tom.

"It sure is," replied Korczak, taking a black case from his pocket. He pulled out and lighted another cigar. "Two enormous beaver live there. We're on pretty good terms these days, but it wasn't always like that." He puffed the cigar, and studied the beaver dam.

"Those beaver came here a few years after I did. I really didn't want them to have that water there, but they thought differently. Every night they would put logs in place to start their dam, and every day I would take them down. This went on for some time, and I was getting sort of angry about it.

"One morning I came out, and buried there among the logs they'd cut overnight with their teeth was one of my best axes. Well, I said to them, 'Beaver, if you want a dam there that badly, I guess you're going to have a dam!' I left them alone after that. Of course they built their dam in no time, and they've lived happily

73

. . . and the beaver lived happily ever after

here ever since. We got along pretty well after that because they understood the deal: they don't take my axes, and I don't take down their dam."

Tom's attention shifted from the valley to the mountain. As they drove on, the boy got his first view of the other side of Thunderhead Mountain. The great difference between the two sides startled him.

The front he had viewed all morning was a sheer rock wall jutting straight up 600 feet out of the forest. From the visitor center it appeared the whole mountain was one gigantic rock. To Tom's surprise, the back was a massive hill with a rock outcropping only at the crest. The lower two-thirds of the rock was buried in the hillside, which sloped steeply up from the valley where they had stopped.

The mountain was so big Tom couldn't believe his eyes. It looked pretty desolate, too. Jagged blast fragments, some the size of cars, were everywhere. Several splintered trees were down. A network of lonely roads tracked up and across the mountain, which was coated with dust like tan snow.

"It looks like a war zone back here," said Korczak, puffing the cigar. "Now you're seeing what most people never get to see. It's too dangerous for them back here now. If the public could see this side, they'd have a better idea of why carving a mountain is no easy thing you do overnight."

"I never thought the mountain was this large," said Tom, shaking his head. "It looks like a volcano went off here."

Korczak laughed. "I never thought of it that way. Remember, I've been blasting on that mountain since long before you were born—for over 33 years. I guess if you put all those blasts together, it would make quite a little eruption.

"Many people still don't understand I'm carving Crazy Horse on both sides of the mountain. It's sculpture in the round. One day the public will be able to drive around here just as we've done. There'll be a large dam where the beaver are, and it will make a large reflecting pool in this valley."

"I saw that this morning on the little model with all the buildings," said Tom.

"It's on the architectural model of the future. This will be like that—Crazy Horse carved on both sides. Actually, I've done more work on the back of the mountain than I have on the front. A lot more, only no one ever sees this side. It was very frustrating in the early years. I'd be breaking my back on this side, but people down below at the studio couldn't see anything happening. They thought I wasn't doing anything. Mother would try to explain where I was working, but it's very difficult for people to understand if they can't see for themselves. I didn't blame them."

Tom stared at the big mountain. He looked puzzled, and finally asked, "How did you go about starting to carve a mountain so big? It looks impossible."

Korczak smiled. "Let me try to put it in terms you'll understand a little better. Tom, did you ever take your Boy Scout knife and try to carve something out of a bar of soap? Maybe a little boat or your schoolhouse or some animal?"

"Once I tried to make a carving of Beans. He's my dog."

"There you go," said the sculptor. "What did you do first?"

"I cut off a bunch of the soap around the edges."

"Exactly," nodded Korczak. "You knew just what your dog looked like, so you took that bar of soap and you cut away some of the edges to sort of block out the rough form of your dog. You trimmed off the excess soap you knew you didn't need."

"I almost didn't leave enough for his long nose," said Tom.

"Did you use the whole bar of soap?" asked Korczak.

"Yes."

"And, when you had him all blocked out, what did you do?"

Photograph showing Tom's view of the "other side" of the Crazy Horse mountain carving-in-the-round. Zeus is parked on the work area from which the horse's leg will be carved. Inserted as a point of reference is Korczak's original marble Crazy Horse scale model.

75

KORCZAK, Sc.©

"I put on his ears and the face."

"After you put on all the features, I'll bet you polished it all up."

"I did," said Tom, frowning. "Only, it didn't look much like Beans. I guess I'm not much of a sculptor." They both laughed.

"Tom, I'm carving Crazy Horse on the very same principle you used to whittle out that little dog. I'm using the whole mountain the same way you used the whole bar of soap. I know exactly what the mountain carving is going to look like because I made that small scale model we just saw. Then, I went up on the mountain and started blocking out the rough form of Crazy Horse by taking away all the excess rock—the same way you took off the excess soap first.

"I'm blasting off from both sides of the mountain most of the rock I know I don't need. Just as you did, I'm being careful to leave plenty for the features. Just to be safe I'm leaving 10 feet of extra rock all around. I can always take it off, but it's a little difficult to put it back on. After I have the rough form of Crazy Horse all blocked out, then I'll start putting in the features by taking off that last 10 feet of rock.

"Instead of whittling on a piece of soap three inches high I'm blasting on a mountain 600 feet high. It may take another 100 years to finish, but it's the same principle you used on your soap dog. Does that help you understand what I'm doing and how I got started up there? For all these years I've been blocking Crazy Horse's rough form out of that big mountain. I'd like to see it all outlined against the sky before I die. We've done it step by step. I'll show you. Let's go up."

When the little jeep started again, Korczak said, "Tom, would you open that glove compartment? See that little in dial there? Turn that to the right. Yes. All the way." A little red light flashed on the dashboard. "That puts us in extra four-wheel drive. Now we're ready."

Tom looked apprehensively at the steep rocky trail angling sharply up in front of them. He swallowed. "We're going to drive up there?"

"Sure. You don't want to climb up, do you? This old jeep is tough. She's never let me down like the other one did. You'll have to hang on, though. I mean really hang on. Here we go."

CHAPTER 10

GOING TO THE TOP

The road up was nothing like the relatively flat, wide road from the visitor center to the bottom of the mountain. This road was very narrow with tall trees close on each side. Tom thought he could reach out and touch them as they passed. He wasn't reaching, though. He was hanging on for dear life. He gripped a little metal handle on the dash. His knuckles were white.

The road got steeper and steeper. The front of the jeep was up so much higher than the back, he couldn't see over the hood. Rocks littered the trail, and the jeep bounced off them and lurched across deep ruts. It was very noisy. The engine rumbled, and the wheels threw up pebbles that clattered on the bottom of the jeep. They jolted across a rut, and Tom thought his head was going to bounce off.

Tom was thinking about the blood on Korczak's jacket, and he remembered the story of how a jeep once had tipped over. He glanced nervously out the back of the open vehicle. He was sorry he had looked back. He knew if he bounced out, he'd roll all the way down—like a snowball.

His eyes were watering from all the dust rolling up. He could taste the dirt on his lips. Tom was sure they would roll as the jeep lurched far over to one side, almost into a big pine tree. Then, it bounced into a rut, and lunged to the opposite side. It was like a little boat being tossed about on angry waves. Tom's stomach churned. He was hanging on as tightly as he could, but every so often they'd hit something that would bounce him up several inches off the seat. He wondered why he hadn't bounced out already.

Korczak shouted over to him, "This is like a freeway! You should see the old road. Nothing like this one. It's a mess." The jeep tilted far to one side again, and Tom could hear the metal straining. He was glad he wasn't seeing the old road. This one was plenty bad enough. He thought for every foot they moved forward, they must be bouncing two feet up and down.

Raising his voice so Tom could hear over the noise of the engine and the rocks clanking underneath them, Korczak said, "I've spent about half my time out here building roads. Nobody knows that, but they're a big part of the work here. I've had to build more than four and one-half miles of roads just to get over

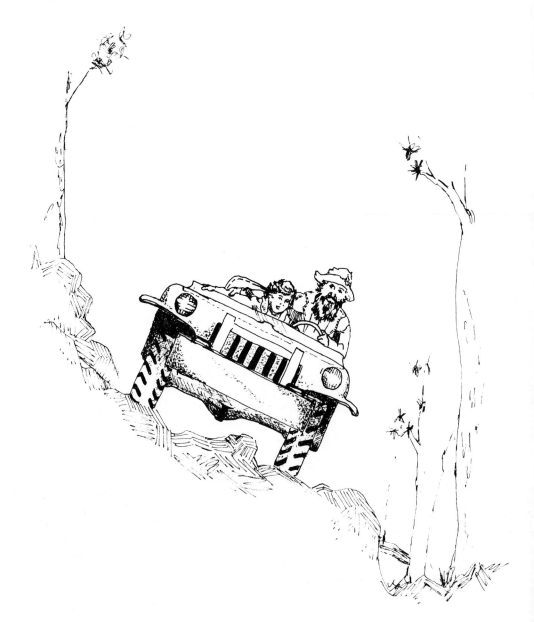

Tom hangs on as the little jeep lurches up the mountain

here and up the mountain. If you figured how many times I've had to rebuild them, it would be many more miles. They wash out every time we get a gullywasher. It's very frustrating to have to take time away from the mountain carving for these roads, but I have no choice. I have to be able to get the vehicles and equipment up and down."

Listening to Korczak, Tom forgot to hold on as tightly as before. They hit a deep rut, and he lost his grip. He bounced over against the side and banged his elbow. It smarted. He grabbed a tighter hold.

Still rising, the rocky road curved ahead of them. Here there were steep embankments on either side of the trail, which looked like the bottom of a dry river bed. "This is what the gullywashers do to my roads," yelled Korczak. "They wash away all the fill, leaving just these rocks. It's hard on vehicles."

"Hard on people, too," thought Tom. He didn't see how they could pass, but Korczak steered the little jeep onto one of the steep embankments. The jeep tilted so severely to one side Tom thought this was it for sure. Gravity pulled him over and pressed him against the door. The passing rocks seemed very close, and he closed his eyes.

The jeep struggled, grinding slowly up and up. Finally, Tom could feel it levelling off. As he opened his eyes, they pulled to a stop on a plateau. Tom took a deep breath.

"Now, that wasn't so bad, was it?" stated Korczak.

Tom gulped. "No, that wasn't too bad." He blushed.

The little jeep idled softly now, and after the noisy climb, it seemed very quiet here. The top of the mountain rose majestically in front of them, and Tom could see the blue sky through the tunnel. They still were in the forest, but he could see down into part of the valley below. He thought they must have climbed up a long way.

"We're about half way up now," said Korczak. Gesturing to another trail disappearing into the trees, he added, "That road you see over there is the original road I built up here 30 years ago. We don't use it much anymore. The one we came up is the third road I've built to get up here.

"This road story—no one would believe it. Besides the four and one-half miles to get over here and up the mountain, I've had to build several more miles down below. I also built that big entry bridge, after waiting 17 years for a permit from the railroad. The Charles Anthony Morss Bridge to Crazy Horse!"

"Was he a friend of yours?" asked Tom.

"One of the greatest friends a man could ever have. He believed in this project when almost no one else did. Without his support I don't know how we'd have gotten through the early years out here." Korczak reflected for a moment, then said, "You hear that noise? Those are the jackhammers. The boys will be finishing up the holes for the blast this afternoon. We'll be going down there, but first I want to show you the top of the mountain."

He put the jeep back in gear, and they moved ahead again. Soon they left the forest, and Korczak turned onto a smoother dirt road sloping gently upward. Tom was studying the big scaffold against the top of the mountain.

"Now you're looking at the other side of Crazy Horse," said the sculptor, "but

81

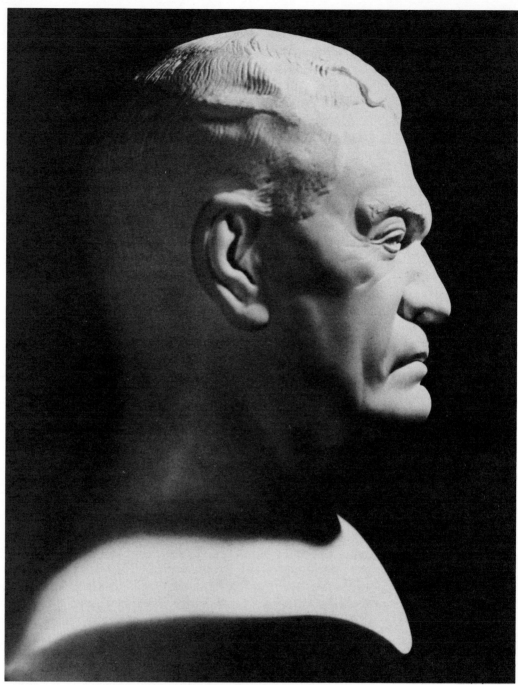

CHARLES ANTHONY MORSS Sr.
The Sculptor's Friend
Carrara Marble   1960-62
Life Size
Crazy Horse Memorial

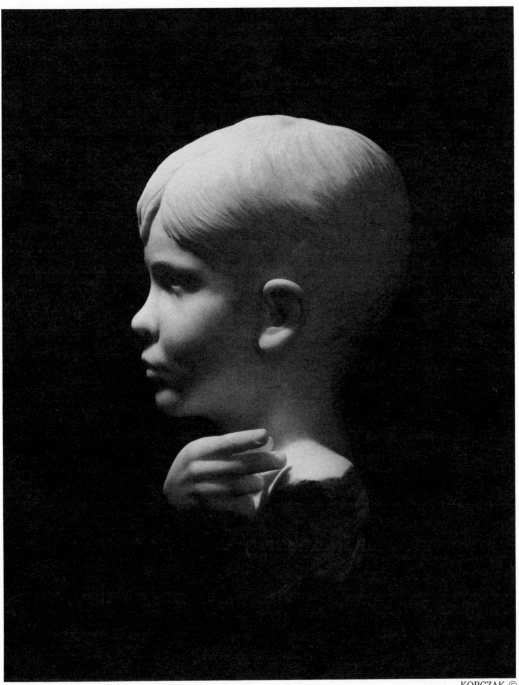

CHARLES A. MORSS Jr.
Six years old
Crestola Marble   1937
Life Size
Concord, Mass.

Building the Charles Anthony Morss Bridge to Crazy Horse

about all you can see from up here is the Indian's head and his arm. We're too high to see much of the horse's head. That's down below us now. It's hard to get much perspective up here. We're too close and the mountain is too big."

"I saw the tunnel from back there, but it's disappeared now."

"It's right above us. You'll see it again when we get on top of this next rise." The jeep passed two roads branching down to the left, but it continued upward. Soon the road became very steep and rocky again. Tom took a firmer hold. He was getting a little used to the bumps now. He could sort of feel them coming, and he bounced with them instead of against them. He thought this jeep ride was a little like learning how to ride a horse.

Gripping the road, the tires threw off a shower of loose rocks that sounded like a hailstorm. The road was so steep Tom again could see nothing ahead but the hood and the top of the mountain almost overhead. It seemed very close.

Suddenly, the jeep levelled off, and Tom was looking directly through the mountain to the horizon far beyond. Tom was startled by the size of the tunnel up close, but before he could think much about it, Korczak hit the brakes. Tom braced himself to keep from flying forward.

"Look! There's our big goat."

As Korczak spoke, a large white mountain goat rose up lazily from where he had been sleeping inside the big tunnel. He shook himself once, and stared at them.

Tom stared back, his eyes wide. He'd never seen a mountain goat before. The animal stood about four feet tall, and had small, off-white horns sticking out of his long head. He had shaggy white fur, thick shoulders and a high, arched neck. His skinny little legs were out of proportion to his bulky body. They looked like miniature stilts.

"That's who really owns this mountain," said Korczak. "He acts like he does, any way. I don't mind. The first day I met that goat many years ago, he was standing in the middle of the road I used then. I wanted to get past him in the jeep, but he wouldn't move. Just stood and stared at me like he's doing now. Only, he wasn't smiling then.

"I came a little closer, and still he didn't move. When I was about 10 feet from him, he sort of shrugged his shoulders, put his head down, and started to paw the ground a little. Now, that's a pretty big goat you must admit. I thought to myself, 'Oh, no. I'm not going to tangle with you up here in your terrain.' So, I slammed the jeep in reverse, and got out of there. I went around another way.

"We've gotten along pretty well since then. He lets me come up here to work, and I don't bother him. He keeps a pretty close watch on me. I'll be bulldozing and look up, and there he'll be, standing in some impossible location on the mountain watching me, like a sentinel.

"There are two of them, and they have a little one about every year. We see them running across the mountain, just little white specks. They can leap great distances and go anywhere. No fear at all. It's amazing they've stayed here with all the blasting, but it doesn't seem to bother them. This big one likes to sleep in the tunnel on a warm day. There's a cool breeze in there in the shade. That's the papa goat. You can tell because he has a distinctive pointed white beard. See it? We've had elk stay in there during a hard winter."

The big goat hadn't moved. Tom was watching him closely. He noticed how majestic the animal stood, like the king of the mountain surveying his subjects. It was a beautiful picture—the white goat framed in the big tunnel with the distant horizon for background.

The "King of the Mountain" rising from his nap in the shade of the big tunnel

85

"I guess we'll have to go all the way up first. Maybe he'll decide to let us in the tunnel on the way back down." Korczak turned the jeep away from the tunnel, starting up yet another steep, rough road. Tom took hold, and glanced back as the tunnel started to disappear from view. The big goat hadn't budged.

Tom definitely was beginning to get the feel of the bouncing little jeep. This time he used his feet as well as his arms to brace himself better in the seat. He worked his legs as he had learned to do in the saddle, letting them act as springs to help cushion each bounce. He narrowed his eyes to a protective slit, and he pressed his lips together to try to keep from eating any more dust.

They were so high now Tom could see the network of roads below them. There seemed to be roads everywhere. He also could see across the valley to other nearby mountains, which gave him his first real sensation of altitude. Still they climbed, the jeep dropping into ruts and bouncing off rocks. Tom wasn't so worried now, and his attention was focused on a low white building perched on the mountain just under the highest rock ridge. A great roar came from it.

Korczak swung the jeep into a switchback curve, cutting the wheels so far they howled. Straining upward, the jeep almost jumped up and around the curve, and came to rest on a grassy plateau beside the noisy white building. He leaned across the seat, and Korczak shouted into Tom's ear, "Those are my big compressors in there. Two of them. You see that pipe running out of the building and down across the mountain? Those big compressors generate air pressure which flows through that pipe. It runs over one thousand feet to where the boys are working below. That air pressure powers the jackhammers and other equipment we use to drill the rock. I'll show you when we get down there."

Tom wanted to ask a question about the air pressure, but the noise was so loud he could hardly hear himself think. He decided to ask the question later.

Korczak put the jeep in gear, and started toward a very narrow ledge that looked as if it had been scratched out of the mountainside. Tom didn't like the looks of it at all. The wall of the mountain rose straight up on one side, but there was nothing but a sheer cliff down on the other side. Tom was very nervous. The ledge didn't look wide enough for the jeep, but Korczak wasn't stopping.

"Ah . . . are . . . we going to drive across there?" the boy stammered.

"Oh, don't worry, I've been coming up here for about 30 years and I haven't driven off yet. This is the first road I ever built up here. I had to build it so I could get my bulldozer on top." The jeep started across the narrow ledge.

Tom knew he could reach out and touch the side of the mountain. The jeep was hugging it so he expected it to scrape the side any minute. He glanced across to the other side, and looked out into space. They now were higher than the surrounding mountains. Tom shuddered, gritted his teeth, gulped, and closed his eyes tightly.

The little jeep rocked along slowly. Tom gasped when he felt it make a little lurch toward the cliff side. His stomach did its own lurch. He gulped again, and kept his eyes shut.

They were on the shadow side of the mountain, and it was cool and calm. Suddenly, Tom felt the warm sun on his face, and a breeze ruffled his hair. Cautiously, he opened his eyes to discover he was on top of the world.

CHAPTER 11

EARLY YEARS ON THE MOUNTAIN

The Black Hills stretched below them as far as Tom could see in all directions. The hills rolled into the horizon like giant blue-green waves. Fluffy clouds dotted the blue sky. Tom thought he could reach up and touch them.

"What a super view!" he exclaimed, forgetting his fear of a moment before.

"I never tire of it," replied Korczak. "You can see into four states from up here. That way is North Dakota. Over there to the west and northwest are Montana and Wyoming, and to the south is Nebraska."

They were parked on a long, flat level of rock about as wide as a three-lane highway. "Do you know where we are now, Tom?" asked Korczak, smiling at the boy.

Tom looked at the giant wooden scaffold next to them. Through the binoculars this morning he had seen a small scaffold on the mountain, but it looked like a toy beside this one. But, he thought, everything was magnified many times on the mountain. Finally he said, "I think we're on Crazy Horse's arm."

"That's exactly right," said Korczak. "We're now on the mountain carving itself, and just below us a few feet into the rock is the Indian's outstretched arm." He pointed to the rock towering up behind the scaffold, and said, "That's Crazy Horse's head. He's just inside that rock. Not very far inside either. Come on, let's go up. I'll introduce you to Crazy Horse."

As they got out of the jeep and approached the scaffold, Tom said, "Those look like wheels from a railroad car."

"They are, my boy," said Korczak. "This whole scaffold stands on railroad wheels that can roll it back and forth on those tracks there."

Tom was amazed to find railroad tracks on top of the mountain. Putting both arms out to balance himself, he walked a track, and asked, "Why does the scaffold roll?"

"I built this scaffold for the finish work on the Indian's head. It's like a giant ladder or a big work platform. We can stand up there and drill holes for the finish work on the Indian's head. When it's time for a blast, we can push the scaffold away to protect it from the blast. It won't have to roll very far because those will be small blasts. Very small. Afterwards, when the dust settles, we can push the scaffold back with the bulldozer against the head to drill more holes. That's why it's built on railroad wheels and tracks. Practical, huh? I'm a very practical man, as you may have noticed.

"I built this scaffold myself in the mid 1960's. It has more than 22 tons of lumber in it. All of it came out of that sawmill we used to operate here. You can see the burner at the end of that big clearing at the other end of the property. It was something to haul all that lumber up here.

"The children loved it when I built this scaffold, especially the young ones. They'd climb all over it, bringing me hammers and nails. We had quite a nice time building it. The children grew up on this mountain. They're like the goats. They have no fear of it. Sometimes that's good, sometimes not so good. You always have to respect this mountain. You never take it for granted."

As they started up a long, steep wooden stairway, Tom remembered how tiny the scaffold had looked from below. Here, it looked like the framework for a house of several stories. Its planks were heavy, and it was very solid.

"Watch your head up here," said Korczak ducking down for a low beam near an opening to the floor above. The scaffold stood about 10 feet away from the rock on the first floor, but on the second floor a large mass of rock extended over to the scaffold. A big white circle was painted on the rock, and Korczak leaned on it.

"Right there is the tip of Crazy Horse's nose. That's the only guess I ever made on this mountain. What else could I do? It's so big. I had to make a stab at it."

"Did you guess right?" asked Tom, reaching out to touch the white circle.

"Fortunately, I was right. It would be pretty hard to start over if I'd been wrong, wouldn't it?" Tom followed Korczak up yet another long flight of steep steps to the third floor of the scaffold. Tom was puffing, and he could feel perspiration on his forehead.

When they stepped through the opening onto the next floor, they emerged at the very top of the scaffold. As Tom came out onto that floor, he froze in his tracks. It was just a flat platform of heavy planks surrounded by a little wood railing. It was if they were suspended in space.

Cautiously, Tom walked over to the railing, and looked down. He was so high it made his head spin. The boy gripped the railing tightly, and said, "I feel like a bird."

"Quite a feeling, isn't it? I spent many years up here. Right up there is where I started in 1948." Tom turned, and saw the mountain rising behind them still higher to a narrow peak. "Where that metal rod is sticking out of the rock at the peak is where I started. That's the top of the Indian's head.

"I noticed you were puffing a little on the steps up. Remember I told you the altitude here is 6,740 feet above sea level, way over a mile high. The air is very thin up here."

Korczak and Tom atop the big four story rolling scaffold

"How did you get up here the first time?" asked Tom.

"Oh, I climbed up. There were no roads at all then. Just rocks to hang onto. I didn't know anything about mountain climbing. I was so naive I wore cowboy boots the first time I climbed up here. You know how slippery they can be. Careful as I tried to be, I slipped and fell about 30 feet."

"Did you get hurt?" Tom inquired.

"Well, of course my pride was hurt. I also banged up my shoulder pretty good. It was the first of many injuries for me up here.

"When I landed, I was on a little ledge, and I just lay there awhile catching my breath. I guess I was thinking mostly about my beautiful home in Connecticut with the lovely lawn and shrubbery, and I was wondering what kind of sucker I was for coming out here to try to carve a mountain for the old Indians. It wouldn't have been too difficult then to go back East. I could have had a wonderful, easy life.

"After awhile, I sort of picked myself up, and said to myself, 'You have a job to do. You don't have any time to lie around being hurt. You promised the old Indians you'd carve a mountain to honor their great Chief, and you're going to keep that promise!'

"So, I started climbing again, and this time I made it to the top. I've had many injuries up here on this mountain since then, but I don't let them stop me. You know, Tom, the world asks you only one question: did you do your job? The answer is not: I would have done it if people had been nicer . . .if I'd had the money . . . if I hadn't gotten hurt . . . if I hadn't died; the answer must be: yes! It doesn't matter what job you do, the answer must be: yes. You don't give up."

"How did you know the right place to start?" asked Tom.

"I guessed," answered the sculptor. "Originally I had planned to carve only the top 100 feet of this mountain. Before I started, I sat out there on a little hill by the parking lot, and studied the mountain. For five days I sat out there watching it in all kinds of light—from dawn to dusk every day. Finally I said to myself, 'Korczak, if you're going to carve a mountain, carve a mountain. Not just the top of a mountain, but the whole mountain. Isn't the story of the American Indian an epic that deserves a truly epic scale? And, isn't it proper there should be one mountain carved as a memorial to the Native American?'

"That's when I decided to carve the whole thing, all 600 feet of it, in the round. Then, I guessed where the nose had to be on a mountain carving that large. That white spot I showed you below. From that guess I knew the top of the head had to be right up there, and that's where I started Crazy Horse."

"How did you get your tools way up here?"

"Carried them up strapped on my back. On that first climb I had a long rope with me. I fastened it to the rocks, and left it there. I used that to hold onto when I went up after that. I needed my arms to pull myself up that rope, so I tied my tools on my back. I'd have my pockets full, too, and something always slung around my neck. I was something to see. It wasn't easy, but I was strong. And, I wasn't wearing cowboy boots anymore! I was much younger then. I was only 40 when I really started working on this mountain."

"I wouldn't want to stand up on that peak," said Tom.

"It is a little airy. You have to be very careful. If a big wind came up, it could blow you right over the edge. That's a 600-foot drop straight down."

Tom glanced quickly down into the valley far below. He shuddered. Korczak continued, "I single-jacked the holes right up there for the first blast on this mountain."

The boy looked puzzled. "Single-jacked? I don't know what that is."

"It's sort of a lost art now. Single-jacking is hand drilling, making each hole by hand. You use a big steel spike, and hit it with a heavy steel hammer. You turn the spike each time you strike it, and it makes a hole in the rock. It's very slow work. Hard on the hands—and the ears. I didn't have any equipment at all then, so that's how I made the first drill holes. There were only four of them, and it took me half a day to pound them out. They were only four feet deep.

"That was for the dedication blast on June 3, 1948. As I told you, that was the only work I did up here that year. Just too much work down below getting ready.

Korczak single-jacking—a "lost art"

I ran a wire all the way from up here down to the studio, and we set off the blast from down there. You could hardly see it, but it took off the first 10 tons.

"It didn't take me long to decide that rope was no way to get up and down from here. That rope climbing with tools on your back and neck gets old pretty fast. So, that second winter, Mother and I built a staircase up the mountain."

"A staircase? From the bottom of the scaffold up to the top of Crazy Horse's head?"

"No. That's only 87½ feet. Remember all this where we're standing was solid mountain then. The staircase ran from the bottom of the mountain down in the valley all the way up 600 feet to the top here. Ah, that was some staircase."

Tom was very curious. "It must have had lots of steps."

"It had 741 steps. I carried up 29 tons of green lumber on my back to build that staircase. That was the winter of 1948-49, one of the worst winters ever in this country. It's in the record books. That was a blizzard with so much snow it came up to the second floor on the buildings in towns around here. Nothing moved for days. It got so cold at night the trees would pop. It sounded like guns going off. The trees would just explode! It was frightening in a way. We got frostbite many times building that staircase.

"We had to fight the elements, too. You always do in this country. If I could work year around, the mountain would be a lot further along. The winters generally are harsh. I don't mind the cold, but the equipment I need up here won't run in the cold. So, we can only work up here a few months a year."

"Can I see the staircase?"

"It's completely gone now. I can show you pictures of it. It was destroyed by the blasting. I used it for many years to get up and down from here. It was still quite a climb, you know—741 steps. I'd usually have to run up and down several times a day. It was a lot better than climbing up on that rope.

A small portion of the steep 741-step staircase Korczak built all the way up the 600 foot mountain

"After I built that first road to get a bulldozer up here on top of the arm, we didn't use it so much. Then, when we started blasting on the Indian's hand and the horse's head, it was all blown away. The big blast fragments smashed it. It had served its purpose.

"I also had a cable car that ran from the valley to about two-thirds of the way up the side of the mountain. You'd have loved to ride in that. It carried a lot of equipment up. That was before the road."

Suddenly, a large bird swooped down on them, and soared out over Crazy Horse's arm. Tom jumped, and said, "What's that?"

Korczak smiled, his eyes trailing the big brown bird floating above the mountain. "That's a golden eagle. They're quite rare now. To the Indians they are good luck omens."

"It's huge," said the boy.

"Yes. Its wing span would be about seven feet. Very graceful in the air. See how it floats there, just riding the wind currents."

"Have they always been here like the goats?" asked Tom.

"Yes, except for once. We had a terrible dry spell, and they went away. I hadn't seen one around here for about 17 years. I mentioned it to an old Indian chief, a medicine man, who was visiting here one day. He didn't say anything. He didn't look at me. To a full-blooded Indian it's disrespectful to look directly into another person's eyes. So, he looked around at the ground, then gazed off into the clouds. Quite a few minutes went by, and finally he said, 'Korczak, in two days the eagles will return. The day after that it will rain.'

"Well, I didn't want to offend him, so I just smiled and nodded. What can you say when someone tells you something like that? After there hadn't been an eagle here for 17 years? Later, I went back to work, and put it out of my mind.

"What do you suppose happened? Two days later I got the shock of my life when five eagles were flying around this mountain. I couldn't believe my eyes!"

"And, did it rain, too?"

"We had more rain than we knew what to do with. I swear it. The next day the skies opened, and it came down in barrels. It rained for four straight days. Did we need that water." Korczak watched the big eagle making wide circles over the mountain. "How did he know? I haven't any idea. Indians are so close to Mother Nature they don't even bother to explain to you. Why should they? We wouldn't understand."

"That's a strange story," said Tom, watching the eagle.

"Oh, I could tell you about so many strange things that have happened up here. You'd find them hard to believe, but I saw them happen. Just like the eagles. The Indians have a special communication with Mother Nature. Other things, too. The Indians say Crazy Horse's spirit is here. I didn't believe them at first, but now I do. Too many things have happened on this mountain since 1948 you just can't explain. Crazy Horse is here. Many people feel him."

Korczak was watching the eagle making wider and wider circles. He wasn't moving a feather, just floating round and round. The sculptor turned to Tom, and said, "I guess I've pretty well introduced you to Crazy Horse. Where we're standing, you're looking almost into his eyes.

"Oh, I know this head doesn't look like much right now, but it will. Remember down below when you talked about whittling your dog, Beans, out of that bar of soap? First, you took away all the excess you knew you didn't need. You said you almost took away too much, and just barely had enough left for the nose. Remember what you're seeing up here is just that first step. I've taken away all the excess, blocking out the rough form—here on Crazy Horse's head, there on the arm, and down below where we'll go later, on the horse's head. I won't start to finish it up until later. That's the second step. First I have to rough it out, leaving enough rock for all the detail work to come after.

"This is going to be some head, you know. It's almost 90 feet high. The whole Sphinx in Egypt is only 70 feet tall. Crazy Horse's nose will be about 30 feet long and his eyes will be about 15 feet wide and nine feet high. I need lots of rock for

An American eagle rides the wind currents above the mountain

all that, so that's why he looks as you see him here today. He's still buried in that last layer of rock, but it's only a few feet thick now."

Tom studied the top of the mountain, and said, "If that's the top of his head up there where you did the single-jacking, it looks like you don't have any rock for the feather."

"Good point," said the sculptor. "You're right in a way. The feather will be the only part not carved from the solid mountain. It will be a man-made obelisk, that's a pillar of stone. The Ancients used to make them. It'll be 44 feet tall. Eleven, four-foot high blocks of cut stone. It'll be free-standing, not have any support but it's own weight."

Korczak had walked over to the opening in the floor, and started down the steps of the scaffold. Tom hesitated before following. Alone, he looked again at the beautiful hills and valleys flowing to the horizon all around. He thought that to stand atop this small platform in the sky was like riding a magic carpet, flying up with eagles.

He put his foot on the first step down, then turned, and looked again at Crazy Horse's massive head. The eagle swooped over it again. Tom felt the air stir. He also felt the mountain. It wasn't just cold rock anymore. Korczak's stories had made it seem alive. Tom smiled, and said softly, "Goodbye, Crazy Horse."

CHAPTER 12

SLOW MAN AT WORK

On the arm at the bottom of the scaffold Korczak was waiting for Tom. They walked over to the edge of the mountain. Looking back, Tom noticed for the first time the big sign on the front of the scaffold. It read, "SLOW MAN at WORK." Tom looked puzzled.

"Go ahead and laugh," chided Korczak. "It's all right. That's what I put it up there for. You have to have a sense of humor in a job like this."

"Does it mean you?" asked the boy.

"Sure. Who else around here is allowed to be slow? I'm the only one who can get away with it! For the first dozen years or so some people said it didn't look like I was doing anything up here. They couldn't see any change. There had been change, but some didn't want to see it. I always say, 'None is so blind as he who will not see.'

"So, when I built the scaffold, I decided to put this little message up here for those people. Some of them still haven't gotten the message." Korczak laughed, and his beard shook like sagebrush in the wind. He reached into his pocket and fished out another cigar, as they walked out along Crazy Horse's arm.

"Are you a football player?" Korczak asked Tom.

"I sure am. I started last year. I'm a receiver."

"That's a very important position. You have to be quick on your feet and with your hands. I played a lot of sports—football, baseball, especially hockey. Bostonians love hockey. You could play a little football up here. This Indian's arm is almost as long as a football field."

You have to have a sense of humor in a job like this," says Korczak

"I sure wouldn't want to try to catch a football up this high," said Tom, shuddering at the thought of the 600-foot dropoffs. They were approaching the middle of the long arm.

Korczak kidded him. "It's nice and safe now. So flat and smooth."

"How long did it take you to get the arm so smooth?"

"I'd have to think. Hmm. It took me five seasons to make that 90-foot cut in front of Crazy Horse's head. To cut a "V" from the peak down to this level where the scaffold stands now, I had to take off 630,000 tons of rock. Those were hard winters, so I could only work up here about four months a year. I was all alone then, too. I'd work the jackhammer from daylight to dark to get as much up here done each summer as possible. I was very strong in those days. That's what gave me this big belly, that jackhammer with 120 to 130 pounds of pressure. You have to push down hard on it to keep it bearing down into the rock, and you push it

96

with your stomach as well as your arms. You develop tremendous stomach muscles over the years. You'll see what I mean when we go below.

"Mother would send a lunch with me. My beautiful horse, Warrior, would be tied to a tree on the back of the mountain. I'd go down for a few minutes, and we'd have lunch together. I'd always have a little something for him. He loved apples. That horse was more human than some human beings.

"It took another seven seasons after that to clear this arm where we're walking. I spent one whole winter just building that road to get the first bulldozer up here on top. The one where I noticed you closed your eyes. Before I got the first Cat up here, I'd push the rocks off by hand. That was no picnic.

Korczak using his stomach as well as his arms to push the powerful jackhammer into the hard rock

"You know, Tom, if you ever did play a little football on this arm, we could get quite a crowd up here to watch. Almost 4,000 people could stand on this Indian's arm."

"Wow! That's a whole army," exclaimed Tom.

"Almost." They were approaching the end of the arm, and Korczak cautioned, "Be very careful now. Don't get too close to the edge. There's no safety net down there, you know."

"I'll be careful." Tom inched forward and peeked over the edge. He looked down 600 feet. In the valley below the tall pines were tiny shrubs. The road they had driven on to the mountain looked like a thin garden hose snaking across a lawn. Tom ducked back from the edge. "That's even more scary than on the scaffold," he admitted. He thought for a moment, then added, "This must be the Indian's hand we're standing on. Is that right?"

"We're right above Crazy Horse's finger right now. His hand is 33 feet thick and his finger is 37½ feet long and 10 feet thick. That's almost twice as thick as you are tall." Drawing on the cigar, Korczak said, "This is where the staircase was. On this end of the mountain. Of course, where we're standing was all solid rock then. Its top step was about 80 feet above us. That was my favorite step—especially when I was carrying up a hundred pounds of tools and dynamite on my back."

Tom peeked over the edge again. "It came all the way up here from down there at the bottom of the mountain?"

"All the way. 741 steps. I counted them many times a day."

"Weren't you scared to be on a wooden staircase running so high up in the air?" asked the boy.

"It was built right against the mountain, so it was solid like the scaffold is now. It had railings, too. No. For me the staircase was a wonderful improvement. Remember, all I had before was that rope I climbed to get up to the top of Crazy Horse's head. After you'd climb that a few times a day, it felt like your arms were going to fall right off.

"Some of my friends didn't care so much for that staircase. It was pretty steep in a couple of places. A group of friends of mine were here one day, and one of them got about halfway up the staircase when he got so scared he couldn't move. He couldn't go up, and he couldn't go down. All he could do was tremble and yell, 'Get me off here, get me off here!' He's quite a famous person, too. You'd know his name I'm sure.

"Do you know what we finally had to do to get him down? One person had to be in front of him and another behind him. He backed down—very slowly. I think he had his eyes closed the whole time. Backed down! Can you imagine? The poor fellow really was terrified, but it was pretty funny, too. Can you picture a grown man backing down a staircase on the side of a mountain?" Korczak and Tom both laughed, and the boy mustered enough courage to look over the edge again. He was getting braver, but the height still made his head spin a little. He stepped back.

"Is this where that cable car came up, too?" asked Tom.

"The bucket? Yes, but it only came about two-thirds the way up the mountain. The cable wasn't long enough to reach clear to the top. Mother and I 'borrowed' that old cable one Christmas morning from an abandoned mine near here. Getting that heavy cable up this mountain was no easy job.

"The cable ran on two big pulleys—one on the mountain and the other in a building about 800 feet out from the bottom of the mountain. I had a beat-up old Chevy engine I used to power the pulley. It ran on gasoline, of course, and wasn't reliable at all. It would stop, and I'd be dangling out there in space waiting for it to make up its mind whether it was going to go up or down. The bucket wasn't very heavy. I built it from lumber. All the equipment I piled in it weighed a lot, though. I'd ride on top of the equipment.

"It could be a little dangerous riding in that bucket. The cable wound on a big spool like thread winding on a bobbin on a sewing machine. Only, the cable was so old and brittle it would all pile up on one side of the spool instead of flowing evenly across it. Sometimes, when I'd be hanging 300 or 400 feet above the treetops, the cable would drop off the spool, and without warning the bucket and all would drop about eight feet. Then, it would swing wildly from side to side until the momentum stopped. Your feet would fly right out from under you. It was just like hitting an air pocket in a light airplane, only there wasn't any seat belt to hold you in that bucket. The equipment would be crashing around when it dropped,

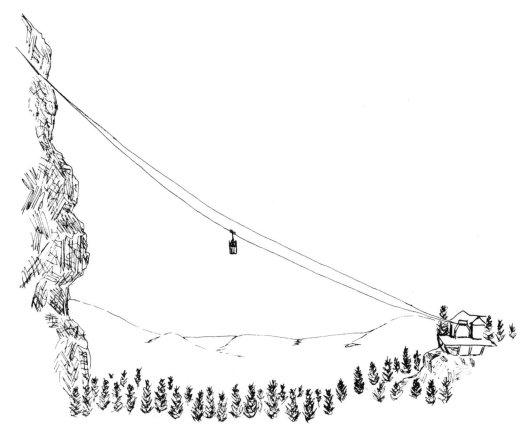

Suspended on its cable 300 feet in space, "the bucket" sways high above the treetops on its perilous journey up the mountain

and you'd have to grab the sides to keep from being thrown out. It would take your breath away. More, if you didn't have a strong stomach.

"Going down could be even more hair-raising. Sometimes the brakes wouldn't work just right, and the bucket would go faster and faster, streaking down the cable. You didn't know if it would stop or not. There were quite a few tense moments. Mother wouldn't go near it. She finally put her foot down, and forbid me to use it. She didn't mind the staircase, though. She helped me build it."

Tom said, "I never thought carving a mountain was like this."

"Neither did I, my boy. Neither did I. As I've told you, carving a mountain is not one thing. It's many, many things, as you're seeing. You learn as you go. Up here, if you don't learn, you're dead. That bucket may seem like a strange thing, but I had to have a way of getting my heavy equipment up here."

"Did you ever make a bad mistake up here?" asked Tom.

"Sure, and it was a big mistake. Of course, on Crazy Horse it would have to be!" He puffed on the cigar, and the wind whipped the smoke away out over the edge. "In the early days before this arm was cleared and long before I made that big model of Crazy Horse, visitors had a very hard time understanding what I planned to do up here. So, I decided to paint the whole outline of Crazy Horse on the side of the mountain. I thought that would help them visualize the sculpture-to-be. Well, painting that outline was the biggest mistake I ever made on this mountain.

"I spent almost a whole summer hanging onto a one-inch rope over the side of the mountain painting it 400 feet above the tree tops. No safety harness or anything. I'd have a gallon of paint tied to my belt and a four-inch brush in one hand. I had to hang onto that rope with the other hand. Why I wasn't killed painting that outline I'll never know. It's another of those things that makes you wonder about this unusual mountain and this project.

"To make the outline clearly visible from the studio a mile away I had to paint the lines about six feet wide. That took 176 gallons of paint for the whole thing, which is a lot of paint with a four-inch brush. If you've ever painted a picket fence, you know what a chore that is. Imagine painting an outline on the side of a 600-foot mountain.

"I also had my old army field telephone tied to my belt so Mother, down at the studio, would tell me where I was on the mountain. I was right on top of it, so I didn't have any perspective at all. From a mile away, she did. Mother would call up and tell which direction to go, whether to go up or down or over this way or that way. She'd say, 'It looks like you should go to the right about one inch and down about an inch.' Well, I had a big photograph of the model with all the exact measurements for the mountain, and I knew if it looked like an inch from down there, it was about 20 feet up here. So I'd go over 20 feet and down 20 feet. Mother would call back, and say, 'That looks about right.' And I'd start painting again."

Tom seemed puzzled. "Why was it a mistake? Didn't it look right?"

"It was a beautiful outline, but people thought that was all I was going to do—just paint. They thought when I finished that outline I was going to pack up

Without even a safety belt, Korczak hangs on a rope 400 feet up the mountain painting the huge outline of Crazy Horse in 1951

and go back East. Oh, I couldn't wait to blast that outline off this mountain. But, everyone's allowed a little boo-boo, aren't they, Tom? Only, why did mine have to be such a big one?"

"I'll bet you didn't wear cowboy boots when you were hanging on the rope that time," said Tom, smiling.

"You'd better believe I didn't. I've had to learn a lot of things the hard way up here, but you don't forget them that way."

Tom looked down on the two blue lakes shimmering in the sun. In the parking lot by the studio-home the sun also reflected off the windshields. "The cars down there look like toys from way up here. It really looks like a small town down there."

"It virtually is today, and it's going to grow and grow. In the early days when I'd blast up here, it was nothing to hit that parking lot with rock. Even a mile away. We had some pretty big blasts up here."

"When you single-jacked?"

"I only single-jacked for that one blast in 1948. We built the staircase that winter, and then I could carry up jackhammers and my steel and bits. In the beginning I only had one old jackhammer. To power it, I bought an old relic of a compressor called a Buda. I only paid $500 for the old Buda. It was such an antique the company that made it didn't even have the records on it.

"Of course, there was no electricity over here then. The old Buda was a gasoline-driven compressor. It only held 35 gallons, and it was always running out of gas. I'd have to fill it several times a day—when I had money for gas. It looked like a boiler on wheels. It was like an old Model A car. I had to hand crank it to get it started. It was a genuine antique when I got it, but it was all we could afford. We were poor as church mice then. $174 isn't much to start a project like this.

101

"I parked the old Buda down there in the valley at the bottom of the staircase because there was no way to get it up here. Then, I built a two-thousand-foot long pipeline around the back of the mountain up to the peak at the top of Crazy Horse's head. It carried the air compression to run the jackhammer 600 feet above. That old Buda was very temperamental, and it was very noisy. I'd crank it up by hand, and run up those 741 steps. I'd just get my jackhammer connected to start drilling, and the old Buda would go 'kaput, kaput, kaput,' and stop. I'd have to put everything down, and run all the way back down those 741 steps. I'd crank it up again, and run all the way back up to the top. Maybe the old Buda would run

Using the Buda was like running an old Model A car

a few minutes, and I'd get a hole about half drilled. Then, I'd hear 'kaput, kaput, kaput,' and the old Buda would stop again. One day I ran up and down those 741 steps seven times. Man, that gets old in a hurry. I was pretty young and strong then, but that running up and down the staircase at this altitude! That would make an old man out of anyone fast."

"Do you still have it? The old Buda?" asked Tom.

"Sure. You can see it down there. It's all painted now. Yellow like everything else. Maybe I should have left it the way it was. It still runs just fine, but it's retired."

Korczak and Tom turned, and started walking slowly back along the long arm toward the little jeep. The sculptor reflected, "Those early years getting

102

started up here were rather unusual. Can you imagine beginning a mountain carving this size with an antique compressor, a beat up old jackhammer and a bucket run by an old Chevy engine? Ha! You don't get much more humble than that. With my modern equipment today I can do in just one year what it took me 15 years to do before.

"It was awfully frustrating those early years, but how else could I start out? I had no money, no equipment, no workers. Standing Bear had promised me all the Indian workers I could use, but I didn't get any. And, there weren't many visitors the first years. In 1948 we had 96,000 visitors. There was no admission then because I naively thought we could finance it with contributions from the people who came in. Do you know what their contributions averaged that first year? Five cents apiece. The next year we charged fifty cents admission. Big deal!

"You couldn't see much of anything up here those first years, except that outline. I'd work alone on top for weeks, and never make a dent you could see from below. It was like that for years. People didn't quite know what to think. I didn't blame them. There is no precedent for anything this large and in the round. There are no comparisons because no one has ever tried anything this big.

"Also, there are a lot of racists around here who hate Indians and anyone else who isn't white. They did everything they could to hinder this project. They still do. That kind of person never changes. They have closed minds.

"But, there were a few believers in those first years. People like Carl Morss. A few. Not many. Slowly, people started coming. Fortunately, I had strong hands and a strong back then, before all the operations. And, I had maybe a little sense of proportion, a feeling for what Crazy Horse could be and mean for the future. I'd promised the old Indians, and I don't give up. Crazy Horse will be."

The sound of the jackhammers pounding far below drifted up, and Korczak said, "Do you suppose our mountain goat will let us in the tunnel now? I'll show you that, and then we'll go down to where the boys are. I still have a lot of work to do this afternoon."

KORCZAK ©

WILD BILL HICKOK
Granite from Crazy Horse Mt. 1951
Created as a gift by Korczak
On the site of Wild Bill's last camp
Deadwood, South Dakota

CHAPTER 13

RUTH'S UNUSUAL BIRTHDAY PRESENT

The goat was gone a few minutes later when Korczak zipped the little jeep into the big tunnel. Tom braced himself thinking they were going to fly right through it and out into space at the other end. Instead, they came to a dusty stop in the middle of the tunnel.

Tom remembered how small it had looked from below. It didn't look big enough to crawl through. So, he was very surprised to discover it was more than two stories high and very roomy. The shaded air was cool and there was quite a breeze. It made Tom think of a wind tunnel.

"Well, my boy, right now you're in the Indian's armpit. I guess it's about the biggest armpit in the world." Korczak smiled. "It looks like the eye of a needle from down there, but already this tunnel is big enough so that two large bulldozers can pass in it. This is just the beginning of it, too. When it's finished, it'll be so much bigger you'll be able to stand a 10-story building in it."

"Wow!" Tom exclaimed. "In here? We have a 10-story building in our town. That's really a tall building."

"When it's finished, it won't seem so much like a tunnel anymore. It'll be just a huge opening under the Indian's outstretched arm. It'll be triangular, framed by the arm, the Indian's chest and the top of the horse's neck."

"Sort of like a big arch?" asked Tom.

"Something like that. Yes."

Having climbed out of the jeep, they walked to the end of the tunnel into the bright sunshine. They both squinted in the glare. To Tom's surprise the mountain didn't end at the end of the tunnel. It was much wider than the tunnel, and the edge of the mountain was some distance away across a wide, rocky plateau. They walked across it, and Tom looked over the edge. They still were several hundred feet up.

Korczak sat down on a large rock as Tom picked up a colorful rock that caught his eye. He perched beside Korczak, and said, "One of the things I was supposed to ask was about the minerals in this rock. Some people in my class collect rocks, and they wanted to know about that."

"There are about half a dozen readily identifiable minerals in this rock," answered the sculptor. "It's pegmatite." Taking the piece from Tom's hand, he continued, "The black is the tourmaline. That's a very, very hard substance that ruins my bits. That sparkling part is mica. You'll see white and rose quartz in it. Here's some white quartz right here. This satiny pink is feldspar. This rust-colored part is iron. There's a lot of that in this mountain. That's one of the reasons it has this unusual color. Of course, there's gold. We see it quite often. Rock collectors love this pegmatite. I made two large portraits from this rock blasted off Crazy Horse—*Wild Bill Hickok* and *Sitting Bull.*

"The geologists say the Black Hills are one of the oldest, maybe the oldest, geological formations on this planet. These mountains are billions of years old. Most mountains are pretty new, and they're still pushing up, growing. This mountain is aging because the Black Hills are so old and weathered. This mountain once was maybe one thousand feet higher than it is today.

"The rock is very solid, though. Better than I'd expected. People have said for years that tunnel is going to fall in. I laugh. Look how much rock I've left up there. Do you know where I go when we have a big blast on this mountain? In the tunnel! That's the safest place up here."

Korczak gazed into the tunnel for a long moment, then said, "Tom, making that tunnel was the hardest thing I've had to do on this mountain so far. It was hard-rock mining at its worst."

"Which end did you start at?" asked Tom.

"I burned the candle at both ends! I built that tunnel in two stages, working from both sides. First, I worked on this side of the mountain, clearing this whole area where we're sitting. The original mountain was very thick. This was all solid rock 200 feet up, all the way beyond the scaffold to the top of Crazy Horse's head.

"I didn't want to have to tunnel through all that rock, so I blasted and bulldozed off about 100 feet of the mountain right here. I actually thinned the mountain by that much. If I hadn't thinned it, the tunnel would have had to be twice as long and twice as difficult to build. It was hard enough as it was. All this rock had to be taken away eventually for the Indian's chest, so I really killed two birds with one stone, so to speak. I thinned the mountain for the tunnel to come and got a start on roughing out the Indian's chest. Then, I started to tunnel through from the back side."

Tom looked up at the Indian's head and the outstretched arm above them. Then, he looked over the sheer edge of the mountain beside them. Puzzled, he asked, "If there was no tunnel, how did you get your bulldozer over on this side of the mountain?"

KORCZAK ©

CHIEF SITTING BULL
From 11-ton block of granite from
Crazy Horse Mt.   1953
Twice Life Size
Sitting Bull's grave
Bank of the Missouri River near Mobridge, S.D.

"It wasn't easy." Korczak shook his head. "I came down from the top up there. I built a road down from the Indian's hand. It ran across what will be the mane at the top of the horse's head. It was pretty steep, and I almost went over the edge a couple of times while I was building it. It's about 500 feet straight down on this side where that road was. There wasn't much room, so I had to use a little Cat instead of the big one I used on the arm up there.

"When I finished thinning, the mountain here was 100 feet wide instead of 200 feet wide. I worked on that thinning for more than a year. Unfortunately, this work doesn't show at all from the studio below. Nobody knows about all this. But, it had to be done. All five of my sons were up here helping me then. Of course, the oldest was only a teenager and the rest were quite small. The littlest ones weren't even as high as the jackhammers, but they tackled them. I think they enjoyed being up here during their summer vacation. I'd be on the bulldozer, and they'd be drilling—or trying to."

All five of Korczak's sons helping him on the mountain carving

"Then you started the tunnel on the other side?"

"Right. We were digging for daylight, and I thought we'd never find it. We came out way up there at the top of the tunnel. You still can see some drill holes. Mountain swallows nest in them now. What a miserable job that was: hot, dirty, noisy, backbreaking. I thought we'd suffocate in there before we ever got through the mountain. My boys were older then, and they helped me. We were like moles in that hole. Of course, it was dark in there, too. You couldn't see, you couldn't hear and you couldn't breathe. Did you ever see a ghost, Tom?"

"I don't think so," said the boy, wide-eyed.

"Well, you'd have thought you were seeing ghosts if you'd ever seen us coming out of that tunnel. We'd be covered from head to toe with that fine, powdered granite dust. We'd be completely white—just like a ghost.

"You can't imagine what it was like in there. It was like a cave that got longer and longer. We had to wear helmets to protect our ears from the noise of the jackhammers echoing off the walls. We wore face masks to keep from breathing and eating too much granite dust. Goggles, of course, to keep it out of our eyes, but you couldn't see anything in there anyway. It was like swimming in mud. And, an oven, too. We'd be soaking wet after five minutes in there. That job couldn't have been worse. Of course, we had to carry out all the rock by hand or in wheelbarrows.

"It took me two years to get to daylight through that solid granite mountain. Two years! Of course, nobody down below could see us working there on the

"Making that tunnel was the hardest thing I've had to do on this mountain—so far,"
Korczak told Tom

109

back. As usual, people thought I wasn't doing anything. Two years just to get to daylight! Mother would be down there at the studio trying to explain to people what was going on, but it was hard for them to understand.

"Then, one day, I went down early. Mother was with the tourists giving lectures on the porch. There was no nice covered porch like we have now. It was all open, and she'd get terribly sunburned. By the end of the summer she could hardly talk, she was so burned and hoarse from trying to explain everything.

"I took Mother by the hand, and we went out to the jeep. She kept asking where we were going, but I wouldn't tell her. We went down what is now that beautiful paved Avenue of the Chiefs in from the highway. It was just a dirt road then. We called it 'oil pan alley' because if you weren't careful, it would take the oil pan right off your car. It was very rustic here in those days.

"When we got to the place where the ticket booth is today, I stopped on that hill and turned the jeep toward the mountain. I pointed at it and said, 'There's you birthday present!' "

"She didn't say anything for a moment, then she beamed. A big tear rolled down her cheek even though she was smiling. It was her birthday, and that was the first day you could see daylight through the mountain. The tunnel finally was all the way through. Of course, it was just a tiny opening. You still couldn't see it from the angle of the studio, but from way out there on that hill you could see the daylight through the mountain. That was on June 26, 1970. It was quite a day. Mother never forgot that birthday present. Neither did I!" said Korczak, wiping his brow.

He glanced down at his watch, and said, "Well, let's go down to the horse's head. The jackhammers are still going, so you can see what's happening right now." He got up and started back toward the tunnel.

Tom followed, saying, "I've really enjoyed learning all about how you started Crazy Horse. I never knew it was . . . well . . . that it was like this. I thought sculpture was something different."

"Well, you're certainly not alone," sighed Korczak. They were back in the cool, breezy tunnel approaching the jeep. "That's what's so difficult to get people to understand. As I mentioned, it's a marriage of mining and engineering at this point to rough out the sculpture. The final work will take a sense of proportion and perspective. There's no better example of the mining and engineering than this tunnel. If everyone could see it the way you have, then maybe they'd have some idea . . . ."

DANCING WITH A JACKHAMMER

Tom felt braver as he braced himself for another roller coaster ride. As they angled diagonally downward across the steep hill on the back of the mountain, Tom studied the Indian's outstretched arm high above. He spotted the Indian's hand where he had stood peeking over the edge. He shuddered remembering the height. They were far below and almost under the hand now.

As they started to curve around toward the front of the mountain, the road suddenly dipped and became much rougher. Tom started to say something, but took a mouthful of dust. There was a cloud of it rolling up from the jeep, but it was whipped away by the stiff breeze that greeted them as they rounded the mountain.

In front of them Tom saw a long, wide, rather flat area where the boys were working. They were almost against the ragged rock wall of the mountain towering directly over them. Parked near were a big yellow bulldozer and several other pieces of equipment.

Korczak drove the jeep to where the boys were drilling. As they approached, the thunder of the jackhammers sounded like a freight train roaring past.

Lifting his voice over the noise, Korczak said, "Now you're on top of the horse's leg. It's about 20 feet below us. It's still buried in the rock, but we're digging it out.

"Right in front of us there is the horse's head. That whole mass of rock you're looking at will be the horse's head. See what beautiful rock it is. Very solid. I couldn't ask for better."

Tom's eyes moved slowly upward. He had to tip his head back to see all the way up. The mountain seemed to be leaning over them. It was a little frightening because there were big chunks of rock above them that looked as if they could come crashing down on them all at any minute.

Korczak saw Tom frowning at the rock overhang, and said, "That's one of the things that makes it so dangerous up here. If some of that loose rock decides to come down, it gets a little hairy. Our motto up here is: 'Don't look up!' We also knock on wood a lot," added the sculptor, rapping his knuckles on his forehead.

Tom said, "It's hard to imagine a horse's head as big as this."

"It'll be 22 stories high. Tom, I've waited many years to work on this horse's head. This is what really excites me. Many other things had to come first, as you've seen, but now I don't care if I do anything else. To make a horse's head like this is the greatest challenge. After all, it is Crazy HORSE." He chuckled, and winked at Tom.

Korczak honked the horn, and Casimir switched off his jackhammer. He ran over to the the jeep, pulling off his yellow hard hat and ear protectors. They left a funny outline in the grey granite dust that covered him.

"We're doing the last three holes here," he reported to his father.

"Good! Let those two finish up there, and you and I will go over and get *Zeus* going. I want to do a little bulldozing while you load for the blast this afternoon. How many holes will we have?"

"With these three, we'll have 20."

"That'll be a good blast." Korczak honked again, and waved for Adam to come over. To Cas he said, "You've done them all at the same angle?"

"Yes, sir."

"Fine. That should clean out this area pretty well. Tom, you'll see a pretty good blast this afternoon. Adam, maybe we can put Tom to work while he's up here. Take him over there and show him what an easy job you guys have up here. Cas, let him wear your hard hat and ear protectors. Okay, kiddo, let's go."

Tom jumped out of the jeep, and he and Adam approached the jackhammers. Adam's stood hissing air, which Tom knew came down through the long pipe from the big compressors far above by Crazy Horse's head. The holes the boys were drilling in the rock were about the size of a silver dollar. The jackhammers stood on steel rods disappearing into those holes in the rock.

Joel had not stopped working his jackhammer. He leaned his full weight over it, pushing the rivoting steel rod into the rock. A steady geyser of powdery granite dust erupted out of the hole, and sprayed the air. The wind caught it, and swirled it away.

When Tom fitted the padded ear protectors over his head, much of the roar was shut out. He put on the hard hat, which came down way over his ears. Adam smiled, and asked Tom if he were ready. Tom read his lips, and nodded.

Adam turned a switch, and the jackhammer jiggled to life. It shook itself, and Tom thought it looked as if it were dancing. Taking hold of the handles, Adam leaned over it, pushing the steel into the rock. Tom could feel the rock at his feet vibrating, and a little geyser of granite dust started to spray up from the hole. Adam indicated to Tom to take hold of the handle, too.

Eagerly, Tom reached for the metal handle, but when his fingers touched it, he jumped back. The handle felt like it was alive. Adam gestured to him to take hold again, and this time Tom started to get a cautious grip on the handle. The harder he tried, the faster the jackhammer seemed to spring away from him. He frowned, and studied Adam leaning heavily on the pounding hammer.

Spitting out more granite dust and squinting to keep dust out of his eyes, Tom grabbed the vibrating handle. This time he leaned into it a little, imitating Adam. The handle started to jiggle out of his hands again, so he tightened his grip and leaned on the handle a little more heavily. He could feel his teeth rattling.

Tom dances with the jackhammer

Tom was hanging on now, but his whole body was jerking up and down like a puppet flopping at the end of its string. He thought his arms and his head would fly off. Finally, he let go.

As he stepped back, perspiration running down his face and his eyes watering from the dust in them, he noticed Adam and Joel both smiling at him. Both still were drilling, but Joel gave Tom a "thumbs up" sign, telling him he had done well. Under the granite dust which pretty much covered him now, Tom blushed. He was very proud to have helped run a dancing jackhammer on Crazy Horse.

Tom moved back from the area where the boys were drilling. He pulled off the hard hat and ear protectors. He was breathing heavily and was very warm. The breeze hitting his moist hair was cooling. He'd just started to catch his breath when he was startled by a roar. It was *Zeus*.

Tom had been so busy with the noisy jackhammers he hadn't seen or heard Korczak start bulldozing. Very curious about *Zeus*, he moved a little closer. Tom thought *Zeus* looked like a big yellow tank. It crawled very slowly, rolling on heavy metal tracks that gripped the mountain like giant claws.

Its powerful engine was very loud, and each time it roared, puffs of jet black smoke shot out of a little smokestack on top of the engine. They made a series of black dots, and Tom thought of smoke signals. When the big blade on the front of the bulldozer scraped across solid rock, there was a screech that pierced like chalk scratching across a blackboard.

In front of the blade was a jagged rock about the size of a small car. The bulldozer strained to move it. Korczak was inching it toward the edge, where Casimir was standing giving hand signals to his father.

The rock didn't want to move. As the bulldozer pushed, the blade would start to slip up over the top of the big rock. It looked as if the blade would high center on it. Each time this happened, Korczak would stop, back *Zeus* up a little, drop the big blade with a thud, and start pushing again. *Zeus* would growl and roar, spit smoke and claw the mountain, inching the rock forward another few feet. Then, Korczak would have to stop again and repeat the cycle.

The big rock seemed to move a little easier as *Zeus* approached the edge. The blade now had picked up a lot of other rocks and gravel, and *Zeus* gave a mighty roar. As the machine struggled forward, Casimir held up his hands, telling his father to stop. The big rock was perched on the very edge of the mountain.

As Tom watched, the whole edge of the mountain started to crumble away. The smaller rocks and gravel sank, and suddenly the big boulder dropped from view. Tom could hear rocks crashing down the mountain. It sounded like an avalanche echoing across the valley far below. A thick cloud of dust mushroomed up like mist from a waterfall.

Tom's heart skipped a beat. The edge had fallen away right up to the big tracks under *Zeus*. The heavy blade of the bulldozer was hanging out in space far over the edge. Tom held his breath. He still could hear rocks rolling down as *Zeus* slowly started backing away from the edge. Tom noticed the smoke now was light grey instead of black, and *Zeus* seemed to be humming instead of growling.

***Korczak hangs Zeus' blade over the edge of the mountain while Casimir helps guide
his father***

Cas ran over to the bulldozer, and hopped up on the tracks. Korczak opened the door of the tall cab, and they talked for a minute. Then, Cas jumped down, and ran over to Tom.

"Father wants to know if you want to ride in the Cat."

"Really!" Tom exclaimed. He hesitated. "Should I?"

"Why not? You ran the jackhammer didn't you? You're going to be sore tomorrow anyway, so a few more bounces in the Cat won't make much difference. You can be co-pilot."

"Okay," beamed the boy, and they ran back to the bulldozer. The tracks were so high, Tom couldn't climb up, so Cas boosted him up by the seat of his pants.

Tom gets a boost up into the Big Cat

116

CHAPTER 15

RIDING A CAT

Korczak opened the door for him, and Tom climbed into the cab. It was quite warm inside, and filled with cigar smoke. Korczak still was wearing the battered hat. "Hello, Tom. Say, how did you like that jackhammer?"

"I had a hard time holding on to it."

"It does try to get away from you. You have to lean hard on it. That's how I got this big belly. It's not fat, it's muscle from all those years of having my stomach pounded by jackhammers. I've lost track of how many years I worked them. Well, what do you think of my beautiful Cat?"

"I've never been in a piece of machinery this big before."

"It is big. Weighs about 72 tons. I've had this Cat for about 30 years. Got it used, of course. Old *Zeus* is my workhorse. I've moved several million tons of rock with it."

The boy said, "We read in school that *Zeus* was the king of the gods. Is that why you call this cat *Zeus*? Because it's king of the bulldozers?"

Korczak laughed, and puffed the cigar. "I never really thought much about it. Maybe it's because *Zeus* could do impossible things, and this up here is sort of an impossible job."

Tom looked around the inside of the cab, and said, "There's no steering wheel."

"It's a little more complicated than that. You work it with these levers here and those big clutch pedals down there. You have both hands and both feet going all the time.

117

"Are you ready for a little ride? See that pile of rocks over there? I want to get that off before this next blast."

"My dad won't believe I rode with you in *Zeus!*"

Korczak smiled, stuck his cigar in his mouth, and started moving the levers and clutches. *Zeus* growled, and the big blade in front began to rise. Korczak eased the big Cat into gear, and the claws took hold. Tom noticed Korczak's eyes were sparkling.

Tom was sitting on a metal box beside Korczak. There was no padding. *Zeus* apparently had no springs. Tom's whole body shook as the big tracks began to roll. He could hear the grinding as the tracks chewed up small rocks below.

When he had watched through the binoculars this morning, it looked to him as if the bulldozer were rolling smoothly across the mountain, almost gliding. Tom was surprised to discover *Zeus* did not roll. The big Cat moved in short jerks over the uneven rock. His body registered each one. He also was surprised the little cab was like an echo chamber. It was noisier inside than it had been when he watched from outside. The engine was so loud it sounded as if they were sitting on top of it. The vibration shook the whole cab.

As Tom stretched up to see out the high windows of the cab, Korczak said in a loud voice, "This used to be an open Cat, but we put this cab on a few years ago. So many rocks were coming down from above. The cab gave me some protection working under the horse's head. At least from the smaller ones. And, it helps keep out the wind and the cold. It's always windy up here like today. Before we put the cab on, I always was catching cold.

"The weather is such a big part of this project. People don't realize what short working seasons we have. I can take the cold. I rather like it, but that jackhammer you ran won't work when the temperature gets under about 38 degrees. When you're this far north at an altitude way over a mile high, it's under 38 degrees much of the year.

"On the average I guess I've only been able to work up here on the mountain about four months a year. Maybe five. If I'd been able to work year around, I'd be a lot further along. We've had only about three open winters since 1947."

Near the pile of rocks Korczak stopped the Cat, and lowered the big blade. As he eased *Zeus* forward again, the engine growled louder, and the smoke turned black. A steady stream of it poured out now. Over the engine Tom could hear metal straining. *Zeus* shuddered, and attacked the rocks and gravel. They spilled up over the top of the blade, and dust billowed all around them. The wind whipped smaller stones back at them, and Tom could hear them bouncing off the big windows. He noticed they were very pockmarked, and one was fractured. Dust seeped in around the doors. Tom coughed.

Suddenly the big Cat lurched to the right, and stopped with a thud. Tom flew off the metal box. He just had time to catch himself before he crashed into the door.

Korczak grimaced. "Oh! That's hard on the back."

"What happened?" asked Tom, rubbing his elbow and shaking the dust off himself.

"This is solid rock we're on, but there's a soft pocket there. Sometimes a blast

118

will take off a little more than we want, but you can't see it because it's full of loose rock. The Cat will sink into those pockets, as we just did. That's what makes this such dangerous work. It isn't so bad here, but over on the edge where it's 350 feet down, a pocket like that can be a little tricky.

"If you think what just happened was bad, you should have been in that bucket when it would drop 20 or 30 feet when you were 300 or 400 feet up in space. That would take your breath away. Mother was right about that bucket, but I'd never let her know that!"

Tom gulped. "I heard a Cat went off the mountain once."

Korczak frowned. "Yes. The D-6, a smaller size than this one. Casimir was driving it, and its brakes failed. He was behind me and a little above me working on the other side of the mountain on the edge of a 250-foot-deep canyon. I heard something strange, and looked back. The Cat went cartwheeling over me and over the edge. I thought, 'Oh, merciful heaven. Casimir has been killed.'

The "Flying Cat" cartwheels through space as Casimir bails out for a safe landing

119

"I stopped *Zeus*, and jumped out. What do you think I saw? There was Casimir sitting on the only soft spot of ground on this whole mountain. Sitting there dusting himself off. He'd jumped just as the Cat went over the edge. How he managed to land on that one soft spot I'll never know. Leave it to Cas.

"Tom, have you every been angry and happy at the same time? That's what I was at that moment. I've never let him or any of his brothers run a Cat up here again. I can take the chances, but I won't let them do it. That was too close a call for comfort."

Tom's eyes were wide. He asked, "Was the Cat destroyed?"

"That's the other strange part of it. We looked down, and there was the Cat at the bottom of that canyon. It landed on its tracks, and it was still running. Black smoke was puffing out of the smokestack as if nothing had happened. It was wedged between a couple of big rocks, but we moved them away, and drove the Cat out the next day. There wasn't a thing wrong with it. Ever since then that D-6 has been known as the 'Flying Cat.' That incident is another of those things you just can't explain."

Working the levers and clutches, Korczak backed *Zeus* up a little out of the pocket, then took another run at the big pile of rocks. "My back is a mess. I've had six discs taken out of my spine in four back operations. When I hit a pocket like that, oh, man, it smarts. But, I don't complain. I laugh, and say I'm a spineless so-and-so. You know, no discs in my spine. Ha! Remember, the world asks you only that one question—did you get the job done? You can't let a little thing like six missing discs slow you down . . ."

Zeus moved on. The billowing dust swirled around them. It was so thick now Tom couldn't see in front of the Cat. It was as if they were flying blind. He was worried because he couldn't see Cas anywhere. It was hot and dirty in the cab, and the noise was deafening. Tom couldn't hear himself think. The metal box seemed to have gotten harder, and every jerk of the big Cat shook his body. He stole a glance at Korczak. The sculptor was concentrating on the levers and clutches.

Zeus was screaming now, the tracks grinding, the big blade twisting, the wind bombarding them with rocks clattering like hailstones on the cab. Tom feared the windows would shatter. Metal was straining and popping all around them. Still *Zeus* roared forward. Tom knew they must be almost on the edge, but he couldn't see Cas for the dust. He shuddered, perspiration streaming down his dirty face. His heart was pounding.

Suddenly, as if they had flown out of a cloud, Tom was looking over the blade into blue sky. He looked down. Under the blade he could see trees in the valley far below. He held his breath. It was much quieter, and he could hear the avalanche of rock crashing down the mountain. For a long moment *Zeus* didn't move. Neither did Tom—not a finger. He knew the bulldozer was suspended on the edge of the mountain, the blade hanging out in space as he had seen earlier.

The falling rock sounded farther and farther away. Then, *Zeus* shuddered again. The little cap on the smokestack bobbed up and down. Grey smoke now. Slowly, they backed away from the edge of the mountain. Tom breathed again.

Korczak stroked a little dust out of his beard, and turned to the boy. "You look a little pale, Tom."

"That was like riding a bucking bronco! Only, I think that would be softer," replied Tom.

The sculptor smiled. "Well, it does have its moments. That was a smooth ride. Some I'd rather forget. Especially up there on top of Crazy Horse's arm."

"I think all my bones were rattling."

"I know exactly what you mean!"

"The dust was so thick. How could you see to keep from going over the edge?" asked Tom. He was still breathing hard.

"Did you ever hear of flying by the seat of your pants? That's what we were doing. It's hard to explain. After all these years, I have a certain feel for where I am on the mountain. The rock and the Cat tell me a lot. Of course, Casimir was there on the edge helping guide me. That makes it a lot easier. I could see him some of the time . . ."

"It sure was rough. Didn't it hurt your back?"

"Sure. It always hurts. It's a funny thing, though. This is the only place in the world I'm really happy. I'm a kid again in this Cat up here on this mountain. I really am. Maybe you can see it.

"I love it up here. I have the most exciting job in the world. No question about it. You have to improvise every day. You work with the rock, and the rock works for you. If you fight it, you're in trouble, big trouble on a mountain this size.

"Does my back hurt after a ride like we just had? Of course it hurts, but I can't stop for every little ache or pain or broken bone or heart attack. I've had two of them up here. Work is one of our greatest blessings. Every man should have an honest occupation, a job he believes in so he can give it his best. Of course, first he has to believe in himself. I believe in myself, and I believe I can do this job, even if I'm getting a little bit old now and pretty battered and bruised. I don't complain. I have my work. And, remember, Tom, I made a promise to those old Indians who invited me out here to carve a memorial to their great chief. It was an unconditional promise. No 'ifs.' I promised I'd do it, and I'm doing it.

"A reporter was up here one day doing a story. He saw what you've seen, and he asked me why I work so hard at my age. I guess he thought maybe I should be retiring or something. Sometimes intelligent people can ask the dumbest questions. I laughed at him. Retire! Now in 1982, I'm only 73, and I have a job to do."

Tom noticed Korczak's eyes were flashing, and his voice had taken on a steely tone. "I have a responsibility not only to those old Indians, but to the people who believed in me. People like Judge Cabot and Mary Lewis, a wonderful teacher I had once. And, great friends like Charles Anthony Morss, Mrs. Comstock and Dr. E. W. Taylor. Those names won't mean anything to you, but they put their faith in me—a little Polish orphan boy from Boston. You don't turn your back on that just because you might get hurt or old or tired or whatever. You do your job. First you have to be true to yourself. 'To thine own self be true,' as Shakespeare said, and then to those who have believed in you. Retire! What kind of a question is that?"

Korczak glared out across the valley, puffing on his cigar. The eagles caught his eye.

"As you've seen, it can be dangerous up here. But, always remember Crazy Horse's spirit is here helping. You see out there? The eagles? Three of them now. They love to ride the wind currents, circling up there while I bulldoze. They watch me almost every day. To the Indian they are a very good omen." Korczak rubbed his back, and added thoughtfully, "I'm awfully glad they're here."

Zeus was humming, and the dust was settling. The sculptor turned to Tom, and said, "I'll bet you'd be surprised if I said you could listen to Crazy Horse."

"What?"

"You can. Let's go over to where the boys are working, and I'll see if I can arrange it."

KORCZAK ©

MRS. BERTHA COMSTOCK
"Beloved by Korczak"
Study in Plaster   1935
Life Size

CHAPTER 16

TOM LISTENS TO CRAZY HORSE

Adam, Casimir and Joel were loading the drill holes for the blast when Korczak and Tom joined them. They had parked *Zeus* around the back of the mountain away from the blast area.

A box labled "dynamite" caught Tom's eye. Korczak told him. "Cas is my dynamite man. He's good at it. He'd better be. If we make a mistake here, poof! It's all over."

"We have almost all the holes loaded." said Casimir. "Just these four left." Tom watched him take a long stick of dynamite from the box. It looked like a giant firecracker. After inserting an electric cap into the dynamite stick, Cas rolled it between his hands and knotted the two colored wires around the dynamite. Using the wires, he carefully lowered the dynamite into the drill hole.

"Those are very powerful explosives," said Korczak. "They're a combination of dynamite and nitroglycerine. That pink stuff is Prill. It's an explosive, too."

After Casimir lowered the dynamite into the drill hole, Adam put a hose in it. It was attached to a small yellow machine Joel operated. It controlled the flow of the Prill, which looked like pink sand. When Joel turned on his machine, the Prill flowed like water through the hose. Adam carefully filled the dynamite-charged hole with the Prill until some of it sprayed up out of the hole.

"Don't waste it!" shouted Korczak. "That's expensive stuff."

Joel quickly switched off the machine, and Adam moved on to the next drill hole Cas had stuffed with dynamite. Tom noticed the little covered wires ran up through the Prill out to each hole.

Casimir loads dynamite in a drill hole

"They make quite a team, don't they?" said Korczak. "It's an unusual story—a father and three sons carving a mountain to a race of people that once lived. Four daughters down there helping their mother take care of the visitors." Korczak had a cigar stuck in his mouth, but Tom noticed it wasn't lit.

"I don't think I'd like to handle dynamite," said the boy.

"It can be very tricky. We have to be sure there isn't any lightning around when we load those holes."

"Will they all go off at once?"

"It will look like one big blast, but actually it will be a rapid series of three blasts each about two seconds apart. The first small one will loosen all this rock here on the surface. The second blast will be a little larger, and fracture the rock down about five feet. Then, the third blast, a big one 10 feet down at the bottom of the hole, should lift out this whole area.

"We've drilled these holes at an angle so the blast will throw the rock toward the edge. I hope most of it will go over. What doesn't, I'll have to bulldoze away. Then we start over again. It's an endless cycle: drilling, blasting and bulldozing."

Casimir had rolled a big spool of heavy wire toward them. He began attaching each of the little colored wires together, then linking them to the big wire he'd cut off the spool.

"You're seeing why carving a mountain is so expensive," said the sculptor. "All this equipment, fuel for it, drilling steel and bits for the jackhammers, and

124

the explosives. This is what that money your class sent gets used for. It would buy maybe a box of dynamite, just like that box we're using for this blast. Or, it might buy one drill bit. We use several of those a day. That's only the beginning of the expenses."

It was getting to be late afternoon now, and the sun was casting heavy shadows on the mountain. The breeze was cooler.

"We always like to blast late in the day," explained Korczak. "That gives the mountain a chance to settle overnight. We're careful not to shake it too much, but often a blast shakes loose some rocks way up above. We'd prefer to have them come down overnight when we're not up here working under them."

"Did rock ever come down on you?" asked Tom.

"Almost. There have been many close calls, but we try not to think about it. I told you our motto."

"Don't look up," said Tom.

Casimir shouted over to them, "We'll be ready in a few minutes."

"All right. Tom and I will take the jeep around to the back of the mountain. Be sure to get all these tools out of the way. We'll see you back there."

As Korczak and Tom walked over to the jeep, the sculptor said, "Moving all the equipment and tools for every blast takes a lot of time, but it has to be done. We can't be too careful. You never know exactly where these rocks will fly."

"How far will the rocks from this blast go?"

"This isn't a very big blast. I'd say maybe half a mile. At least that. Sometimes they'll go exactly where you want, but other times . . ." He rolled his eyes. "I've lost track of how many times we've knocked down the power lines way over there. Then, we lose time because we have no electricity up here until we can get it fixed."

"Did anybody ever get hit?" Tom asked.

Korczak gave a low whistle. "We had a TV crew here once that wanted to be close to the mountain for a blast. I told them it was too dangerous, that they'd have to get their pictures from the visitor center.

"Finally, they picked out a spot about halfway to the mountain. I didn't want them there, but they argued and argued. They said how they'd taken pictures in war zones and in riots. Oh, they'd been everywhere. I said, 'All right, but you'll have to take your chances—and you'd better be ready to duck or jump behind a tree.'

"It was one of our largest blasts. Huge chuncks of rock erupted out of that mountain. It did sound like a volcano going off that time. The rocks flew right toward us in a high arc. It was frightening. I yelled for them to watch out. Just as I ducked down, a great big rock went hurtling past me. I'd have been killed on the spot if that rock had hit me. A smaller rock did strike one of them. He got quite a bruise on his arm.

"That TV crew couldn't get over it. They said it was worse than any war zone they'd worked in anywhere. That was a close call. Too close. Now, I won't let them that close no matter how much they insist."

"Did they get some good pictures?"

"Sure. Wonderful pictures, but every time they showed them, those TV people just wanted to run for cover."

They had parked the little jeep next to *Zeus*. Soon the boys joined them in another jeep loaded with tools. Getting out, Korczak gestured toward a small grey box with a handle sticking up out of it, and said, "That's the detonator. That's what sets off the blast."

"We're all ready," said Casimir. "Shall I call down?"

"Okay," replied his father as Casimir picked up a two-way radio. "We always call Mother. We don't want her to worry. She likes to tell the tourists so they can have their cameras ready."

"Is this where we'll be for the blast?" Tom asked uncertainly.

"It's very safe here," said Korczak. "We're far enough around the mountain. The blast will go the other way. Would you like to set off the blast?"

Tom was so surprised he didn't know what to say. His eyes got wide. "Ah . . . could I?" he stammered.

"Sure, but first I have to tell you a little story. After I'd worked up here the first few years and some strange things had happened, I got to wondering if Crazy Horse might really be inside that mountain. So, one day at a time just like this, I said to him, 'Crazy Horse, are you in there? Crazy Horse, do you hear me?' Then, I pushed that handle. There was a great roar, and I knew he was in there waiting for me to dig him out.

"I'll bet you can hear him, too. Just take hold of that handle, and ask him if he's still in there."

Tom pushes down the detonator, listening for Crazy Horse

126

Tom hesitated. He looked up at Korczak, who smiled, and nodded for him to take the handle. Tom took hold, and called out, "Crazy Horse, are you still in there?"

Tom felt Korczak gently press on his hand, and Tom pushed the detonator handle down. The next moment was like the Fourth of July. The mountain exploded, spraying rocks that skyrocketed in high arcs trailing dust behind them like streaking comets. The ground shuddered, and there was a great boom, like a bomb going off. Tom listened, and thought sure he could hear Crazy Horse's answer."

The mountain above them disappeared in a thick cloud of dust. Tom could hear rocks raining down on the valley on the other side of the mountain. Thud, thud, thud.

It was over in a minute, and silence returned as the dust cloud drifted away on the wind.

"Well?" asked Korczak. "Did you hear him?"

"I think I did." Tom beamed. "I sure think he answered me."

Korczak and the boys smiled. "Okay, fellows. Let's go down and take a look."

They took both jeeps, but could not drive to where they'd parked before. The whole area was strewn with big and little jagged boulders. There was a deep crater where the blast had been. Cas came over as his father studied the crater.

"Looks okay," said Cas.

"Yes. I wish it would have taken more over the edge. There'll be quite a bulldozing job in the morning. I don't want you boys working under the horse's head any more today. We'll let everything settle overnight. There are some pretty big rocks up there.

"Why don't you get the crowbars and see if you can push over some of those big ones on the edge. I'll get the rest of that with the Cat tomorrow. Be sure to call Mother to let her know everything is all right."

Korczak started the jeep, and Cas joined his brothers to return to work. "Mother worries about us up here. She'll always be looking through the binoculars after a blast to see us come down to check. When she sees us, she knows we're okay."

"That blast sure was loud," said Tom.

"I hope it didn't scare Adam's cows too badly. A few years ago we had a very big blast, and all the cows ran off. They went for miles. We never did find two of them."

They were heading around the back of the mountain. Tom asked, "How much rock did that blast take off?"

Korczak stroked his beard with one hand. "I'd say approximately eight thousand tons. It was a smaller blast. From down there at the studio you won't be able to see any difference at all. It's frustrating. That's why the sign says, 'Slow Man at Work.' I'm slow, but I'm steady. Over the years all the little changes add up to big ones. Today it's encouraging that after all these years people can see it all beginning to be outlined against the sky. Even strangers."

Tom was thinking about the big blast he had set off. Although they were bouncing as much as before, the road down the mountain didn't seem as rough to him as it had on the way up. "I thought the whole mountain was going to come down when that blast went off," said the boy.

"There's a funny story about those blasts. Sometimes you can feel them for miles around. One day Mother got a call from a little old lady who lives on a small ranch about five miles from here. She was very polite, and said, 'Mrs. Ziolkowski, the next time your husband is going to set off one of those big blasts on Crazy Horse, if it wouldn't be too much trouble, I'd appreciate it very much if you could let me know a few minutes in advance. You see I have a wonderful collection of plates in my China closet, and every time your husband sets off one of those blasts, it shakes some of my plates off the shelf.'

"Can you imagine feeling a blast that far away? Sometimes Crazy Horse answers more loudly than other times!"

The little old lady with her "rocking" china closet

128

CHAPTER 17

"MAY HIS REMAINS BE LEFT UNKNOWN"

Once off the mountain and again on the level road back to the studio complex, Korczak asked, "Would you like to see my tomb?"

Tom was startled. "Ah . . . well . . . I never saw a tomb before." It sounded scary to Tom.

"Come on! We can stop off on our way back to the house."

Korczak took a turnoff that led them parallel to the front of the mountain. Tom noticed in the later afternoon sun the mountain was changing color again. It looked rustier.

They rode on through tall pines until Korczak said, "You can see it there at the bottom of that big rocky knoll."

The rock outcropping above Korczak's tomb on which the permanent Indian museum will be built

Tom tugs to open the big door on the tomb

A little distance in front of them Tom saw what looked like a cave at the base of a large rock outcropping about three stories high. The cave had a rust-colored door with lettering on it. They dipped down through a little draw, and as they approached the tomb, Tom could read the letters. They said:

KORCZAK

Storyteller in Stone

May His Remains Be Left Unknown

Korczak parked the yellow jeep, and they got out and walked up to the big door. Tom could see drill marks in the rock around the door, and he realized it was not a cave.

"The boys and I worked seven winters blasting this tomb out of that solid rock," explained Korczak. "We worked on and off here in this little protected draw when there was too much snow and cold to do anything else around here. We'd drill and have a small blast. When the weather would clear up, we'd do other things—like build roads."

Tom walked over and touched the letters on the door. The largest were about a foot tall. "Storyteller in Stone," read Tom.

"That's all I am," stated the sculptor. "I hand cut those letters out of three-quarter-inch steel. They told me it couldn't be done, but there it is. That last line has 26 letters, just like the alphabet. I like that. Go ahead, you can open the door."

Tom looked at the tomb apprehensively. Cautiously, he took hold of the big handle. He could barely get his hands around it. He pulled, but the door didn't budge. He tugged harder. Still it wouldn't move. Then, he put one foot up on the doorjam, and strained with all his might. The door moved a fraction of an inch. Tom glanced over at Korczak, who watched but said nothing. So, Tom took a deep breath, and yanked the door as hard as he could. This time it popped open several inches. Tom could feel cool air escaping from inside. He shuddered.

Korczak said, "The boys and I hung that door ourselves. It weighs about a ton, but you didn't have too much trouble opening it. I'll bet you never moved a ton before. Now you can swing it with one finger."

Tom was surprised to discover the big door did move very easily now. He smiled, and pushed it open with his finger.

The afternoon sun splashed inside, and illuminated a room about twenty by thirty feet. The low ceiling and walls were solid granite and the floor was smooth concrete. A rectangular metal box stood in the center of the room, which otherwise was empty.

Korczak walked into the tomb. Tom hesitated, then followed. It was quite cool inside.

"The temperature doesn't vary much in here. It stays cool like this year around. It's like a good wine cellar. I have a friend who calls this my potato cellar!" Korczak's laugh bounced around the room.

131

Tom walked over and peeked inside the heavy metal box. It was empty.

"That's my sarcophagus," said Korczak. "My casket will go inside, then this steel lid here will roll on top of this metal box, and it will be sealed. Pretty cozy, isn't it?"

Tom wasn't so sure. He didn't know if he liked the idea of being in a tomb.

Korczak continued, "The boys and I made my casket a couple of years ago. It's just a simple wooden box. Pine. I didn't have anything when I came into this world, and I don't want anything when I leave it. You know, I've never taken a salary or expense account at Crazy Horse in all these years. Never. But, I do want to be here."

In his "potato cellar" Korczak tells Tom about his sarcophagus that won't float.

Tom tried to roll the lid of the sarcophagus, but it was very heavy. Korczak gave him a hand, and the steel rolled onto the metal box. It fit perfectly. "That's very heavy steel. It's one inch thick. I didn't want it to float if we ever get a flood here." They pushed the lid back on its rollers.

"You've seen I'm a practical man, and I think it's a very practical thing to plan for the future. Saves everyone a lot of bother later. Plus, I know exactly where I'll be. I'll be here with Crazy Horse. Everyone will know if they don't continue this project, I might come out and get after them!

"All this must be continued, Tom. Crazy Horse is for the future. Maybe my being here somehow will help see it through. So, I think this tomb is a practical matter."

Tom had relaxed a little, and as he looked around the spacious room, he said, "I always thought a tomb would be scary, but this is sort of nice, I guess."

"Mother didn't think much of it when I started it. She's gotten used to the idea now. She wouldn't have a thing to do with it the first few years we worked here. Finally, she decided I was going ahead with it anyway. One day she said, 'Well, Korczak, I guess it's like carrying an umbrella. If you carry one, it doesn't rain.' After that she didn't seem to mind so much. Now, I think she agrees with me it's a practical thing."

"Has she been inside here?" asked Tom.

"Ha! Not for the first seven years. She wouldn't even come over here and look at it. Then, she'd come to that little hill over there where I first pointed it out to you. Finally, she came inside the day the tomb was consecrated by the Catholic Church. This is an official cemetery plot around the tomb.

"Our dear friend, Father O'Connell, came one beautiful April morning to consecrate the tomb. He conducted a wonderful ceremony right inside here. We had a row of chairs, and eight of the 10 children were here. That lid we rolled was the altar, and the altar cloth was a beautiful beaded Indian prayer given to me by the Iroquois Indians. They were the ones that gave me that unusual drum in the Museum.

"Mother came that day. We weren't sure she'd come inside, but she did. It was a very memorable day for all of us."

Tom could hear birds singing outside. As they turned to leave, he stopped abruptly, and said, "What's that?"

"Meadowlarks."

"No. That on the door?"

"What does it look like?"

"It looks like a door knocker."

"That's what it is. A brass door knocker. Jadwiga gave it to me."

"But, it's on the inside of the door." Tom looked puzzled.

Korczak smiled. "I put it there so if I ever want to come out, all I have to do is knock. It's just a little touch of humor. You have to have a sense of humor. When Mother heard about that, do you know what she said? 'Well, I suppose the next thing you're going to tell me is you want a telephone in there, too!' Oh, I loved that. But, you know, Tom, it isn't such a bad idea, is it?"

He put his arm around the boy's shoulder, and they walked slowly out of the tomb. When Tom pushed the heavy door, it closed with a thud of finality.

He studied the legend again, then turned to Korczak, and said, "I don't understand what that means—'May His Remains Be Left Unknown.' "

"I thought a long, long time before I decided on that. What it is telling people is to never forget that the story of Crazy Horse is the important thing, not the storyteller. Sure, I want to be here and be a part of this always, but the story in stone on that mountain is what this is all about. Not Korczak. 'Life is short; art is long.' That mountain is so the world will never forget a race of people apart from us that once lived here. The legend on that door is a reminder not to confuse the story with the storyteller. That's what it means."

The shadows were growing longer, and the breeze had picked up. The tops of the pines swayed, and Tom could hear their gentle murmur. It sounded like a distant river. The clouds now had a touch of pink, and, looming above them, the mountain was rustier than before.

"I always hate to leave the mountain and the forest to go home. I'd rather stay out here. It's so peaceful. Don't you feel that? No wonder these hills are sacred to the Sioux Indians. I think when the white man came he must have been a little jealous of the Indian because he had such a beautiful country. Not just here, but this whole nation. The Indian had a rich life.

"Isn't it funny how we work 30 or 40 years so we can retire and enjoy the great outdoors? Hunting or fishing or gardening? The Indian had those things from the day he was born until the day he died."

They climbed back into the jeep, but Korczak didn't start it. He seemed lost in thought, gazing up at the mountain.

"Look. There's a deer watching us," said Tom, pointing to their right. About twenty feet away stood a big buck with a large set of antlers. "He's so still. He looks like a statue."

"There will be others nearby. They're on their way to the lake. The wildlife will start appearing everywhere now. That whole area there to our right is where our Boy Scout trail runs. It's a five-mile nature and historical hiking trail. Young people, not just Boy Scouts, come here to hike it, and study the plants, animals and rocks. Then, they can go in the Indian Museum, and see how the Indians made beautiful and practical things from the materials they found in nature.

"That's why the Nature Gate we're making is going to be such a fitting entrance to Crazy Horse. All those gleaming brass animals, birds and plants. You cannot separate Nature and the American Indian. They lived as one."

The low sun was spotlighting the rock where the tomb was and the mountain as it had done when Tom had first seen it in the morning.

Korczak said, "When Crazy Horse is almost finished, the permanent Indian Museum will be built right on top of that big rock outcropping where the tomb is."

"The hogan?" asked Tom.

"You know about that?"

"Your wife showed it to us on the little model this morning. The one with all the buildings that will be here in the future."

"It will be a very unusual building, and this will be a wonderful setting for it. You'll be able to look out through that big circular opening in the roof of the museum and see Crazy Horse looking down. It will be very dramatic. People will come here from all over to learn about the American Indian."

Korczak started the jeep, and its noise broke the hush of the pastoral setting around them. "I suppose we'd better be getting back. Mother will be wondering what happened to us, and I imagine your parents will be here soon to pick you up. It certainly has been nice having you visit."

They started back on a road leading to the parking lot where Tom and his family had arrived that morning. Korczak said, "This is another road I built dur-

Korczak tells Tom, "The Indian lived as one with Nature."

ing winters when I couldn't work on the mountain. This is the other end of the Avenue of the Chiefs you came in on this morning. One day this part of it also will be paved, and it will be lined with stone statues of famous Indian chiefs from all the tribes of North America. The public will drive all the way to a new parking lot by the hogan."

As they approached the studio, Korczak detoured around the parking lot and drove up a grassy knoll a little distance away and above the parking lot where Tom had arrived. From there they could look down on the studio-home complex and across the valley to the mountain carving beyond.

"This is my favorite spot to look at the mountain," said the sculptor, stopping the jeep and killing the engine. "See how it's framed against the sky."

HURRICANE BILL
Two Views
Maple   1931
Wing Spread: Six feet
Crazy Horse Memorial

CHAPTER 18

"MY LANDS ARE WHERE
MY DEAD LIE BURIED"

The eagles are still there," said Tom, watching the three big birds still circling on the wind currents over the mountain. "The forests do look blacker now."

"The Hills turn a deep purple towards evening. We're going to have a beautiful sunset in a few minutes. That's what I wanted you to see, the sunset on the mountain. Notice it has changed to that interesting coppery color."

"It seems to change color all the time," said the boy.

"That rock has great character. It's never the same color. You know, the pigment of an Indian's skin changes, too. When they are in the forest, their color is a deep reddish copper. Inside a room, their color is lighter. Outside in their natural environment, it's much darker, richer. I've always noticed that with full-bloods."

"The mountain seems to be glowing," said Tom. "I can see the outline you're blocking out very clearly now. Crazy Horse's head, the arm, where the horse's head will be."

Photograph of the Crazy Horse mountain carving on which Korczak's line drawing, which is in proportion to the actual mountain, shows how much rock is left to be removed. Approximately seven million, two hundred thousand tons of granite have been removed from the mountain at the time of this picture.

137

KORCZAK, Sc.©

"I'm very pleased you can," said the sculptor. "This is where I sat for those five days before I started the mountain carving, when I decided to carve the whole thing. If I'd have done just the top 100 feet instead of the whole 600 foot mountain, I'd have finished it long ago. But, I made the right decision. I have no regrets. I knew then I couldn't finish it. This project is for the future."

Tom said, "When I look up at that big mountain, it's hard to believe I was way up there on top with you. Getting to run the jackhammer and riding in *Zeus* with you. What an adventure!

"Did you ever wish you'd picked a different mountain?"

"Never. If I'd searched the whole world, I could not have found a better mountain for this purpose. Look at the light on it now. In the dawn it's gold; in the evening, a dying ember. That parallels the history of the American Indian. It's as if Nature is helping me tell the story. Look at the motion that the lay of the rock gives that mountain. I couldn't have found a more perfect mountain than this one. And, now I'm sort of glad it's in the Black Hills. The old Chiefs were right about their Paha Sapa."

Korczak took another cigar from his black case. After he'd lighted it, he said, "There's something almost mystical about that mountain. About the whole story. Many Indians believe that. I didn't in the beginning, but I do now. Too many things have happened you just can't explain—like that story of Crazy Horse and the stone.

"During his lifetime Crazy Horse always wore a stone at his ear. It's in my model, and it will be up there, too. When anyone asked Crazy Horse about that stone, he always would say, 'I will return to you in the stone.' When I first heard that, I didn't believe it, but it was repeated to me by those who knew Crazy Horse. When those five survivors of the Battle of Little Big Horn were here for the dedication in 1948, I asked each of them about it. They had known Crazy Horse personally. They had fought with him. Each one said that story was true. They saw him wear the stone, they heard him say, 'I will return to you in the stone.' How can you explain a thing like that, Tom? You might as well not even try.

"It was wonderful to have those five old men here. Five of the six survivors. They had the most marvelous faces and beautiful names: Comes Again, Pemmican, High Eagle, Iron Hawk and Callous Leg. The youngest one was 88. They told me all about Crazy Horse. What he looked like, what kind of man he was. They were in awe of him, spoke almost reverently about his bravery. They confirmed everything I'd heard and read. Five separate first-hand accounts, an oral history lesson for me.

"I explained the non-profit humanitarian concept to them, through translators, of course. They would talk quietly among themselves, gesturing, nodding and smiling. Then, one would tell me what the group thought. Those old survivors thought it was just perfect that this would never be a federal project. They liked that very much.

"They loved the concept of the Museum and the University-Medical Training Center. To them that part was just as important as the mountain carving. It was always so curious and such a disappointment that Standing Bear never understood the humanitarian side.

"I guess I am about the only white man the Indians ever invited out here, and I promised them I'd carve their memorial. There was no question in their minds who should be on that mountain. It should be Crazy Horse. Before I started, there were some suggestions that some other Indian leader should be up there. The tribes held a big meeting down on the Pine Ridge, and they hashed it all out. In the end, they voted it should be Crazy Horse. No one ever has come up with any good reason why it shouldn't be Crazy Horse.

Five survivors of the Battle of Little Big Horn attending the 1948 dedication of the mountain carving described Crazy Horse and told Korczak a great deal about him.

"There's another story like the stone at Crazy Horse's ear that you can't explain. September 6th. That's the day Crazy Horse died in 1877. Well, that's the same day I was born 31 years later. September 6th. Some people have said Crazy Horse died on the 5th of September. That's the day he was stabbed in the back by a white soldier while he was at Fort Robinson under a flag of truce. He didn't die until the following day, September 6th. My birthday.

"I'd say it was just a coincidence, but the Indians don't. They say I was born to carve that mountain. To the Indians, that date is an omen. They say I was meant to bring Crazy Horse back in the stone, the way Crazy Horse said he would return. Isn't that amazing, Tom? I don't argue with them anymore. How can you explain it? I can't. The Indians do, though. They have no trouble with it at all. Curiously, it was another 31-year cycle until Standing Bear invited me out here."

"It's very mysterious," said the boy.

"It is indeed. Just like that mountain. Look at how intense the color is getting now. It will get just a little redder as the sun starts to dip over the horizon.

"A full-blooded young Indian man worked with me once on that mountain.

141

He was a veteran who had done many brave things in the Air Corps. He made dozens of dangerous jumps. He worked with me one day up there. At the end of the day he came to me and said, 'Korczak, I have to leave. I can't work on that mountain anymore.' I was very surprised. When I asked him why, he said, 'Because the spirit of Crazy Horse is up there on that mountain.'

"I didn't question it. I didn't understand it, but I didn't argue. He went away. This was a very strong young Indian who wasn't afraid of anything. Had proven it many times. But his beliefs about the mountain were too powerful. He couldn't work there. How do you explain these things? There have been many other things like that over the years. I never was superstitious before I came out here. I am now. Why have I not been killed in all the close calls in 34 years on that mountain? I've been a razor's edge away from death up there dozens of times. Just like Casimir. How could he have landed on the only soft spot of earth up there when the Cat flew over the edge? You just can't explain those things."

"Did you ever meet any other Indians who knew Crazy Horse?" asked Tom.

"Yes. Just one other. Black Elk. I met him the first year I was here. I also met Mari Sandoz. I told you about her fine book about Crazy Horse. She came from Nebraska, and she spoke Lakota. She lived near the Indians for many years. She was a friend of He Dog, who was Crazy Horse's great friend.

"I met her in New York once, and we talked a long time. I asked her what there was about his young Indian, Crazy Horse, that made him such a remarkable person. She said to me, 'Korczak, he must have had an unbelievable charisma. That means a very dynamic presence. The only way I can describe it is with a story He Dog told me:

" 'The year after the Little Big Horn—that would make it the summer of 1877—Crazy Horse's followers knew they were going to their death. The buffalo were gone, and there was no way for them to get food. The federal troops were after them from all sides, so there was no time to rest. The followers were not only the braves, but the mothers, children and grandparents. The Indians knew they would have to surrender, but they were waiting for Crazy Horse to come back. He had gone off alone, as he always did.

" 'Then, one day they saw this lonely figure coming on a broken-down horse, and they knew it was Crazy Horse. Their hearts were lifted, and everything was wonderful. It didn't make a bit of difference if they were going to die. The effect his presence had on them was so strong they forgot everything else. They were happy. He had that greatness.'

"When Mari Sandoz told me that story, she got all choked up the way I do when I talk about Crazy Horse. There's no question that he was a truly remarkable person. Please read her book about him."

Puffing his cigar, looking out at the glowing mountain, Korczak again seemed lost in thought. After awhile, he turned to Tom, and said, "Well, my boy, you've had quite a day. I hope I've answered most of your questions. Have I?"

Tom beamed. "Oh, the stories have been very interesting. I've learned so much. I didn't know much about Indians . . . and, I guess, I didn't know anything at all about mountain carving." Tom thought for a minute, then added, "I guess I have one question you haven't talked much about. In school we read how you wouldn't take money from the government. We didn't really understand why you didn't want it. You needed the money, didn't you?"

"Oh, merciful heaven, yes! The mountain would be looking much better today if I'd had more funds. You've asked a very key question, Tom. It's right at the heart of this project. Let me try to explain it to you this way:

"Why should a memorial to the American Indian be financed by the very government that broke its treaties with the Indians and turned its back on all its promises? Wouldn't that be lip service—hypocrisy pure and simple?

Korczak tells Tom about the humanitarian goals

"Isn't it better that a project like this be financed by the interested public that pays a small fee to visit here? I never wanted to charge a fee, but I had to. You've seen how expensive it is to carve a mountain. We never charge an Indian or anyone in military uniform. We have open house twice a year so area people come here free of charge to see the progress and the changes.

"I'm a great believer in the free enterprise system. That's what made this country great, Tom. Only in America could a man carve a mountain. Only in America. So, isn't it right that this memorial should be paid for by those people who pass on the road down there, and want to come in here? Nobody stands down there and twists their arms. They come because they want to come. They know what this is. I think that's the way it should be, instead of being paid for by the taxpayer, who doesn't really have any choice in the matter.

"That's one reason I didn't want this to be a federal project. Free enterprise can do it. I've proven it. There's another very important reason.

"My biggest frustration on this project for all these years has been trying to get people to understand this is much more than a mountain carving. This is a non-profit humanitarian project to and for the American Indian. I must have said it a thousand times. Two thousand times. But, Crazy Horse is a very romantic figure and the mountain carving is a very dramatic thing. People get all wrapped up in those, and forget the rest of this project. Of course, some of them won't see because they don't want to. I didn't come out here to build a tourist gimmick. I came out here to build a humanitarian project, and that's what I'm doing. The mountain is pretty far along now, the Indian Museum is started, and we've established all those Indian scholarships. That's a pretty good beginning.

UNIVERSITY

INDIAN MUSEUM

AVENUE OF
THE CHIEFS

PRESENT STUDIO HOME
AND INDIAN MUSEUM

MEDICAL TRAINING CENTER

KORCZAK, Sc.©

Korczak's detailed, long-range plans for Crazy Horse are illustrated in this painting showing how his nonprofit humanitarian project will look in the future when its major goals are accomplished. Those goals are: (1) the mountain carving, (2) the Indian Museum of North America, and (3) the University and Medical Training Center for the North American Indian. Stone portraits of famous American Indian Chiefs will line the Avenue of the Chiefs leading through the University-Medical Training Center complex to the 350 foot-in-diameter Indian Museum near the base of the Crazy Horse sculpture in the round.

"But, I told you a few minutes ago this project is for the future. Tom, it's a sad fact most people live only for today. They don't live for tomorrow. Crazy Horse is for tomorrow. When I sat here back in 1948 and decided to carve that whole 600-foot mountain instead of just the top of it, I knew this project was much bigger than any one man's lifetime. That's why in 1948 I established the non-profit Crazy Horse Memorial Foundation. Its members will work with my family after I'm gone to insure the continuity and completion of this project. That's why I drew up all the plans for the mountain carving—three books of them. Mother has them. Everything else is all laid out on that architectural model you saw this morning. That is the future, just as you saw it there. That's the humanitarian side—the Indian Museum of North America and the University and Medical Training Center for the North American Indian. This is not just a mountain carving, but even Standing Bear couldn't understand the humanitarian side.

"Now, Tom, do you think the federal government would come in here after I'm gone and finish the mountain carving and carry out those humanitarian goals? Ha! It would never happen. No, sir. It would end when I'm gone, and that cannot be allowed to happen. It must go on, Tom, for the future.

"That's the second reason I turned down the federal money. Twice, I turned down ten million dollars for this project. I'd turn it down again today. Ten times ten million. Oh, it might hurt a little, but I'd do it in a second. There's an interesting little story about that:

"A U.S. Secretary of the Interior came here one day. He stood in my room, and told me he could get ten million dollars for Crazy Horse. He said he'd draw up an iron clad agreement guaranteeing Crazy Horse would be finished and the humanitarian aspects would be carried out.

"You know what I told him? I said, 'Mr Secretary, right behind you on that shelf is a book with about 375 treaties the government made with the Indians. Those were iron clad treaties, but the government broke every one of them. No, thank you, Mr. Secretary. The government's track record isn't so good when it comes to anything to do with the Indians. You can keep your ten million dollars.' Tom, I think he was shocked."

Korczak puffed slowly on his cigar. His eyes were steely. He paused for a long moment before continuing. "You've seen it takes many skills to carve a mountain. It's curious how everything in my life has been training for this job. Being an orphan, growing up in foster homes, working on the Boston waterfront, knowing Judge Cabot, working with Gutzon Borglum, carving the *Noah Webster* statue, landing on Omaha Beach, meeting those old Indians, seeing the vandalism of my sculpture out here.

"The Indians say everything in life is a circle. Well, everything in my life has been training for this project. If Crazy Horse isn't finished, my whole life will have been wasted. The only way I could see to help insure it is completed was to keep it out of the hands of the government and the bureaucrats. They'd have me holding a committee meeting to decide on every blast. Can you imagine?

"Sure it will take a long, long time to finish it. There are two thousand miles of surface on that mountain carving. If it takes another hundred years, what difference does that make? Isn't everything relative? The mountain will be there long after we're gone. It still will be telling that remarkable story of a race of people that once lived. As that wonderful old Indian, White Antelope, said, 'Nothing lasts—only the earth and the mountains.'

"What happens after I'm gone? I'm like a jackhammer. When a jackhammer wears out, you throw it away and get another one. I am only the means. This project is much bigger than I am. You know, in ancient times it was nothing for generation after generation to work on one statue or building. It took over 600 years to build the Cathedral of Notre Dame, and it still isn't finished. People forget those things.

"Crazy Horse is a beautiful idea, and it can go on. Based on the free enterprise system, it will. If this country survives, and I pray it will, this project will survive.

"Tom, those are the reasons I turned down the federal money. I know I can't explain it very well, but I hope that helps you understand it. I did it for the future because Crazy Horse is for your generation and your children's children and all those who come after . . . .

"What you said in the dining room after lunch was a very astute observation. You said, 'It's like history.' You are exactly right. Our treatment of the American Indian is the blackest mark on our nation's history. If Crazy Horse will give back to the Indian some of his pride and create the means to keep alive his culture and heritage, my life will have been worthwhile. To do that is quite an honor for a Polish orphan boy from Boston. Quite an honor!"

The mountain now gleamed reddish-copper against the darkening sky. Studying the changing light, Korczak continued, "When Crazy Horse is finished, the people who come here from all over the world will pay that small fee, and it will finance the humanitarian part for centuries to come. A poem will be carved up there beside the Indian and his horse to help tell the story. See all that rock to the left of the figure? The poem will be carved there in letters three feet tall. You'll be able to read it from here. I hope it will help people understand."

Tom asked, "Did you write the poem?"

"I worked 17 years on it. That's almost a year for each line. I told you I was slow—but steady. There's a lot to be said for the long-distance runner. He usually goes the distance. The poem goes like this:

When the course of history has been told
Let these truths here carved be known:
Conscience dictates civilizations live
And duty ours to place before the world,
A chronicle which will long endure.
For like all things under us and beyond
Inevitably we must pass into oblivion.

This land of refuge to the stranger
Was ours for countless eons before:
Civilizations majestic and mighty.
Our gifts were many which we shared
And gratitude for them was known.
But later, given my oppressed ones
Were murder, rape and sanguine war.

Looking east from whence invaders came,
Greedy usurpers of our heritage.
For us the past is in our hearts,
The future never to be fulfilled.
To you I give this granite epic
For your descendants always to know:
'My lands are where my dead lie buried.'

Before them the mountain now blazed crimson in the setting sun, majestic against the darkening sky.

From the parking lot a horn sounded, and they turned to see Ruth wave at them from beside Tom's parents' car. Korczak said, "Well, Tom, I've enjoyed so much having your company today. You greet your classmates for me, and tell them how much I appreciate their help. Tell them the story of Crazy Horse." The sculptor paused, then added, "I tell my children: When the legends die, the dreams end; when the dreams end, there is no more greatness."

Korczak shook hands with the boy. Tom jumped out of the little yellow jeep, and said goodbye. Korczak winked at him, and said, "Son, don't ever forget your dreams. Never forget your dreams."

THE END

CHRONOLOGY OF MAJOR EVENTS IN THE PROGRESS AT CRAZY HORSE MEMORIAL

A non-profit humanitarian project in three phases:
    (1) the mountain carving,
    (2) the Indian Museum of North America and
    (3) the University and Medical Training Center for the Indians of North America

1939   Summer: Korczak Ziolkowski, Boston-born sculptor, works at Mt. Rushmore as assistant to Sculptor Gutzon Borglum. Fall: Sioux Chiefs ask Korczak to carve a mountain for them. The Indians choose Crazy Horse.

1940   Sculptor comes to S. Dak. from Conn. Meets Chief Henry Standing Bear; makes clay model of Crazy Horse.

1942-43   Korczak sculpts 13½-foot high memorial to Noah Webster as gift to West Hartford, Conn.

1946   Korczak serves in the U.S armed forces in Europe during WW II (landed on Omaha Beach). Decides to accept the Indians' invitation. Indians insist the Memorial be in their sacred Black Hills. The sculptor and Standing Bear search the Black Hills for the *"right"* mountain.

1947   Korczak arrives at Crazy Horse May 3rd with $174 left; lives in a tent, builds the original log cabin studio-home. Korczak is 38.

1948   Dedication ceremonies June 3rd attended by five survivors of the Battle of Little Big Horn. Sculptor "single-jacks" holes for the first blast, which removes 10 tons. Crazy Horse Memorial Foundation formed August 16th. Korczak digs wells, builds roads, works on studio-home. Winter: he builds 741-step staircase to mountain top (elevation 6,740 feet above sea level).

1949   97,000 tons blasted off (horizontal cut for horse's lower mane). Sculptor works alone with a jackhammer powered by a gas compressor (the old Buda) at foot of mountain. Connecting pipeline runs 2040 feet up and across the mountain. IRS makes Crazy Horse Memorial tax exempt November 28th.

1950   Works second summer on mountain (mane cut). Thanksgiving Day marries Ruth Ross. First admission fee 50¢ per adult (1948-49 contributions average 5¢ a person visiting the studio). Builds 32 foot addition to veranda.

1951   Korczak paints outline on mountainside. Six-foot wide lines take 174 gallons of white paint.

1952   Starts cut for Indian's profile. "Bucket" (run by antique Chevy engine) working to take supplies to top of horse's head. Electric compressor now at base of mountain.

1953-55   Sculptor cuts down below Indian's nose. Purchases first "Cat" bulldozer. Chief Standing Bear dies. Korczak turns down $10 million from federal government. Crazy Horse Foundation purchases 328 acres at mountain from federal government. Modern milking parlor begins operation. Architectural model delivered at Crazy Horse. Admission to 75¢ an adult.

1956   630,000 tons removed to date. Korczak works all winter on road up back of mountain to top. Moves Buda compressor up on arm (shorter airline gives more power). Now able to use wagon drill as well as jack-hammers and jack-leg.

1957-58   300,000 tons cleared from arm. Constructs Avenue of Chiefs (gravel) direct from port of entry to studio-home. Lumber mill begins operation.

1959-60   395,000 tons removed (1,325,000 to date). Sculptor has first Cat working on top (more rapid progress clearing arm). Korczak breaks right wrist and thumb.

1961-62 475,000 tons removed from arm. Korczak again turns down $10 million dollars from federal government. Builds sunroom and workshop, roof over visitor viewing porch, large garage and machine shop. Drills new well for studio-home. Sculptor gives his mahogany portrait of Chief Standing Bear to President John F. Kennedy. Crazy Horse School opens. *Korczak's first spinal operation (two discs removed).*

1963 200,000 tons removed (2,000,000 to date). Finishes clearing Indian's arm. Blasts new road to top of horse's mane. Builds theater.

1964-65 350,000 tons removed from top of horse's mane and Indian's pointing finger. Builds 26-ton scaffold on tracks in front of Crazy Horse's face. Korczak makes 16-ton (1/34th scale) plaster model of Crazy Horse and finishes poem he will carve on the mountain. Drills 377 foot deep well. Modernizes public restrooms. Admission fee $1.00 for those over 15. *Korczak's second spinal operation (one disc removed).*

1966-67 450,000 tons removed from upper mane and Indian's chest (2,800,000 to date). Electricity to top of mountain and first electric compressor taken all the way up. Charles A. Morss Bridge built at entrance to Crazy Horse. Road and parking lot blacktopped. Builds octagonal dining room. *Korczak's third spinal operation (two discs removed).*

1968 First cut into tunnel (75,000 tons removed). *Korczak has slight heart attack.* U.S. Post Office open April 1st at Crazy Horse (57730). Charles Eder's Indian Collection and Ebell's Egyptian furnishings given to Crazy Horse.

1969-70 325,000 tons removed (3,200,000 to date). Tunnel under Crazy Horse's arm through the mountain. Korczak purchases D-9 Cat and acquires new compressor, air trac, huge cat-drill-compressor. Eight of Korczak's marble portraits vandalized at entrance to studio-home. Sculptor receives honorary Doctorate from Fairfield University, Conn. *Korczak has massive heart attack.*

1971 200,000 tons removed. Korczak enlarges tunnel and begins roughing out the horse's head. Out of debt for first time. Korczak begins his tomb near base of mountain.

1972 200,000 tons removed. Very dangerous bulldozing at top of horse's head. Winter: sculptor and sons build Indian Museum and new restrooms. Additional water system including new well and drain field. Admission to $4.00 a car.

1973 200,000 tons removed. Museum opens May 30th.

1974 300,000 tons removed (4,100,000 to date). Upper half horse's head roughed out. New road on back of mountain. Indian collection of Chief Luther Standing Bear and Sunflower given to Korczak. Sculptor receives Trustee Award from National Western Heritage and Cowboy Hall of Fame.

1975 500,000 tons removed. First road cut from back of mountain around to face of mountain. Much heavier blasting. "Flying Cat" incident. Korczak bulldozes with right foot in cast after operation to remove a large spur and repair separated Achilles tendon. He builds 80-foot long, 24-ton boom, hoist and metal platform-work cage for finish work on horse's head.

1976 500,000 tons removed (5,100,000 to date). *Reader's Digest U.S. Bicentennial Book* ranks Crazy Horse "one of the seven wonders of the modern world."

1977 600,000 tons removed. Heaviest blasting of the project. 100th anniversary of death of Crazy Horse September 6th, Korczak's 69th birthday; Crazy Horse Centennial blast (largest of the project) removes 40,000 tons at one time. 30th anniversary of Korczak's arrival at Crazy Horse May 3rd.

1978 500,000 tons removed (6,200,000 to date). 30th anniversary of dedication of the mountain June 3rd. Korczak celebrates his 70th birthday blasting and bulldozing—as usual!

1979   300,000 tons removed (6,500,000 to date). First cut into mountain toward horse's nose. Two new roads up back of mountain. 40th anniversary of Standing Bear's invitation to Korczak to carve the mountain. Korczak's tomb nears completion. Indian Scholarship Program begins educational phase of the humanitarian project. Concord Stagecoach (circa. 1856) acquired. Two collections donated to Indian Museum. Tashunka Witco Nature and Historical Trail mapped out (as Boy Scout Eagle Project).

1980   250,000 tons removed (6,750,000 to date). Further cutting into mountain for horse's lower head and nose. Two new roads on back of mountain. One week after his 72nd birthday, *Korczak has fourth major back operation and removal of a sixth disc,* but he works through the open winter. Korczak acquires second D-9 Cat (Jupiter), builds first phase of Crazy Horse Village with new 206-foot well (14th), designs new wing for Indian Museum, designs and begins building 50-foot Nature Gate, hand cuts steel letters for the legend on his tomb: KORCZAK—STORYTELLER IN STONE—MAY HIS REMAINS BE LEFT UNKNOWN. Tomb is consecrated. Admission fee to $5.00 a car. Logging operation resumed. Christopherson oil portrait of Korczak unveiled. Crazy Horse Indian Scholarship Program provides 32 scholarships in first academic year (1979-80)

1981   450,000 tons removed (7,200,000 to date). Seventh million ton removed on 34th anniversary of Korczak's arrival in the Black Hills May 3rd. Sculptor roughs out horse's left eye and constructs 20-foot steel templet for finish work on the eye. Open winter, 1980-81 accelerates progress on emerging horse's head. First road downward across scarf of mountain completed to under horse's nose. New road built on back of mountain. Visitation tops one million for first time. Design for Chief Crazy Horse 13¢ U.S. postage stamp unveiled Sept. 6th, Korczak's 73rd birthday. He receives Honorary Doctorate from Black Hills State College for his sculptural work and his humanitarian concept for Crazy Horse. Indian scholarships total more than 100; scholarships expanded into nursing field. Mountain carving featured on cover of Northwestern Bell Telephone Book for S. Dak. Nature Gate set in place. Two major wells deepened (including original 1947 well). Logging and post operation continue.

1982   First actual sculpting on Crazy Horse as Korczak begins carving the horse's left eye. (Dimensions of just the eyeball: taller than a two-story building, approximately 30-feet wide, and bulging out from the mountain some 18-feet.) First use of the torch to cut rock on the mountain. Jan. 15th, first of an estimated ONE BILLION Crazy Horse 13¢ regular U.S. Postage stamps released as part of the U.S. Postal Service's Great Americans Series. South Dakota Legislature unanimously adopts a special resolution recognizing and endorsing the high honor paid to Crazy Horse by the U.S. Postal Service. *CRAZY HORSE and KORCZAK: The Story of an Epic Mountain Carving* by Robb DeWall published May 3rd, commemorating the 35th anniversary of Korczak's 1947 arrival in the Black Hills to begin his non-profit humanitarian Crazy Horse project.

Additional information on Crazy Horse Memorial can be obtained by writing :
Crazy Horse Mt.
Avenue of the Chiefs
Crazy Horse, S. Dak. 57730

BIBLIOGRAPHY

Armstrong, Virginia Irving, ed., *I Have Spoken*, Swallow Press, 1971, Pocket Books, 1972.

Brininstool, E. A., *Crazy Horse*, Wetzel Publishing Co., Los Angeles, CA, 1949.

Brown, Dee and Schmitt, M. F., *Fighting Indians of the West*, Charles Scribner's Sons, New York, NY, 1948.

Brown, Dee, *Bury My Heart at Wounded Knee*, A Bantam Book, Holt, Rinehart and Winston, Inc., 1970.

Brown, Vinson, *Great Upon the Mountain: The Story of Crazy Horse*, MacMillan Co., 1971.

Burnette, Robert and Koster, John, *The Road to Wounded Knee*, Bantam Books, 1974.

Casey, Robert J., *The Black Hills*, The Bobbs-Merrill Co., Inc., New York, NY, 1949.

Casey, Robert J. and Borglum, Mary, *Give the Man Room*, The Bobbs-Merrill Co., Inc., New York, NY, 1952.

Clark, Robert A., *The Killing of Chief Crazy Horse: Three Eyewitness Views*, The Arthur H. Clark Co., Glendale, CA, 1976.

DeLoria, Vine, Jr., *Custer Died for Your Sins*, The MacMillan Co., 1969.

DeWall, Robb, ed., *Storytelling in Stone*, Korczak's Heritage, Inc., Crazy Horse, SD, 1981.

Garst, Shannon, *Crazy Horse: Great Warrior of the Sioux*, Houghton Mifflin Co., Boston, 1950.

Howe, M. A. DeWolfe, *The Children's Judge, Frederick Pickering Cabot*, Houghton-Mifflin, Co., 1931.

Hubbard, Margaret Ann, *Thunderhead Mountain*, MacMillan Co., 1952.

Kotzwinkle, William, *The Return of Crazy Horse*, Pictures by Joe Servellow; Farrar, Straus and Giroux, 1971.

McGillycuddy, Julia B., *McGillycuddy Agent: A Biography of Dr. Valentine T. McGillycuddy*, Stanford University Press, 1941.

Mails, Thomas E., *Sundancing at Rosebud and Pine Ridge*, Center for Western Studies, Augustana College, Sioux Falls, SD, 1978.

Meadowcroft, Enid L., *The Story of Crazy Horse*, Grosset and Dunlap, 1954.

Miller, D. H., *Custer's Fall*, Duell, Sloan and Pearce, New York, NY, 1957.

Murray, Gilbert, *A History of Ancient Greek Literature*, D. Appleton and Co., New York, NY, 1897.

Neihardt, John G., *Black Elk Speaks*, illustrated by Standing Bear; originally published 1932, reprinted by University of Nebraska Press, Lincoln, Nebraska, 1961.

————, *A Cycle of the West*, originally published by The MacMillan Co., 1915-1949, reprinted by University of Nebraska Press, Lincoln, NE, 1963.

Orlowski, Jozef, *Paderewski*, Carl O. Jevert and Associates, Chicago, 1952.

Sandoz, Mari, *Crazy Horse: Strange Man of the Oglalas*, University of Nebraska Press, Lincoln, NE, 1961.

Smith, H. Allen, *We Went Thataway*, Doubleday and Co. Inc., Garden City, NY, 1949.

Standing Bear, Luther, *Land of the Spotted Eagle*, originally published by Houghton-Mifflin, 1928, reprinted by University of Nebraska Press, Lincoln, NE, 1975.

Warfel, Harry, *Noah Webster, School Master to America*, The MacMillan Co., 1936.

Witt, Shirley Hill and Stan Steiner, eds., *The Way*, Vintage Books, 1972.

Ziolkowski, Ruth, ed., *Korczak Ziolkowski, Mountain Carver*, Korczak's Heritage, Crazy Horse, SD, 1982.

INDEX